Praise for *The BrandPromise*®

"As the world's largest owner of private golf and dining clubs, we strongly recommend the 'BrandPromise Philosophy.' Without a genuine promise most businesses are likely to find themselves merely a commodity."
—Eric Affeldt, President and CEO, ClubCorp

"Genuine Brands begin with passion and a promise; The BrandPromise *is the practical guide to accomplishing both."*
—William L. Eldien, President and Chief Executive Officer, Nolet Spirits U.S.A./Ketel One Vodka

"Successful brands are built by people who understand and embrace the BrandPromise Philosophy."
—Michael Gehrisch, President and Chief Executive Officer, Destination Marketing Association International

"If you're really sincere about creating a personal brand, The BrandPromise *is your key to success."*
—Annika Sorenstam, President, ANNIKA

"It's more important than ever for nonprofits to make a promise. The BrandPromise *provides the roadmap."*
—David Williams, President and Chief Executive Officer, Make-A-Wish Foundation of America

*"*The BrandPromise *should be required reading for every nonprofit and member-owned organization. There's nothing more important than making a promise!"*
—Henry Wirz, President, SAFE Credit Union

"The BrandPromise methodology is fundamental for communities that strive to create exceptional destinations for visitors, businesses, and residents."
—Rick Antonson, President and Chief Executive Officer, Tourism Vancouver

THE
BRANDPROMISE

How Costco, Ketel One, Make-A-Wish, Tourism Vancouver, and Other Leading Brands Make and Keep the Promise That Guarantees Success!

DUANE E. KNAPP

New York   Chicago   San Francisco   Lisbon   London
Madrid   Mexico City   Milan   New Delhi   San Juan
Seoul   Singapore   Sydney   Toronto

1 2 3 4 5 6 7 8 9 0   DOC/DOC   0 9 8

ISBN 978–0–07–149441–0
MHID   0–07–149441–3

BrandMindset®, BrandPromise®, Brandictionary®, BrandScience™, BrandPsychic™, and BrandStrategy™ are trademarks of BrandStrategy, Inc. All other trademarks are the property of their respective companies. These and other easily recognized brands and brand names are used for illustrative purposes only; no sponsorship, association, or affiliation with BrandStrategy, Inc., is intended or implied.

For readability and ease of reference, the BrandPromise® methodology is referred to alternatively as *promise*.

McGraw-Hill books are available at special quantity discounts to use as premiums and sales promotions, or for use in corporate training programs. To contact a representative, please visit the Contact Us pages at www.mhprofessional.com.

This book is printed on acid-free paper.

CONTENTS

Chapter 3

The Roadmap to a BrandPromise Commitment   51

Chapter 4

Promises Are Delivered by People, Not Policies   79

Chapter 5

Five Ways to Keep Promises   101

Chapter 6

Predicting Brand Success   121

Chapter 7

Community Brands: The Destination BrandPromise   141

Chapter 8

Personal Brands   171

Chapter 9

Specialized BrandPromise Applications   203

Chapter 10

Promise Perspectives: The Detailed Process for Building Genuine Brands   233

FOREWORD

A promise is a commitment or pledge made to assure the recipient that he or she can trust that certain expectations will be fulfilled. It goes beyond a simple statement of intent to a higher ethical level that puts at risk the grantor's honor and integrity if the commitment goes unfulfilled.

At Starbucks, we have long been guided by a promise, known internally as our "purpose." Our *purpose* is to provide our customers with an uplifting experience that enriches their lives—the "Starbucks experience." The consistent fulfillment of our purpose is the essence of the Starbuck's brand. It is what our customers expect of us and the reason for their loyalty and emotional connection to the brand, as well as the foundation for our success. For those of us responsible for fulfilling our commitment, it is our common purpose that is widely shared at all levels of the company. It gives us direction, inspires us, and unleashes our passion and commitment to convert our intentions into reality.

As consumers, we are constantly promised that we will be inspired by the food and beverages we consume, the products and services we buy, and the organizations that serve us. The organizations that actually fulfill these commitments gain our trust, our loyalty, and our business. In our other roles as members of organizations of all types, we want to be inspired by a common purpose, the work we do, and the integrity with which we do it. We want to be part of responsible organizations that meet or exceed the commitments they make so that we have reason to be proud of what we do and where we work. Promises made and fulfilled are the foundation not only for consumer loyalty but also the passion, commitment, and loyalty required to create and maintain successful organizations.

In *The BrandPromise,* Duane Knapp provides the insights, strategies, and mechanisms for people who sincerely desire to make meaningful promises that inspire the loyalty of their customers and fellow associates. The BrandPromise philosophy is perfect for individuals and organizations that want to build genuine brands or relationships that are trusted and admired. It requires a sincere and real commitment to customers', associates', and shareholders' well-being and satisfaction.

Making a real *promise* means caring about others in a way that is heartfelt and not just a great business proposition. In a world where companies', products', and even a person's brand equity can come and go like shooting stars, the *promise* offers a practical guide to long-term success.

There is an enormous difference between talking about a promise and making and keeping a promise to customers, associates, and shareholders. The *promise* philosophy focuses on the difference between slogans or taglines and putting your heart and soul into your promise. This book is the definitive guide to understanding, developing and delivering a genuine promise to energize any brand; personal, business, or nonprofit.

One of the greatest insights in this book is that organizations that make a genuine BrandPromise must first decide how they want all their stakeholders (customers, associates, shareholders, influencers, etc.) to feel. Once a brand's "emotional" strategy has been developed, it can move forward with its "functional" (products and services) strategy. It isn't sufficient for a new product or service to produce profits; it must also enhance the customer's emotional connection to the brand.

As dramatic changes in technology and innovation continue to affect everyone's lives, there is an increasing opportunity for individuals and organizations to distinguish their brands by providing exceptional experiences that customers can count on and enjoy. After all, a brand is only as good as its promise!

Orin Smith
Chief Executive Officer (retired)
Starbucks Coffee Company

PREFACE

Imagine a world where everyone makes a promise and keeps it. The reason for the BrandPromise book is to provide a practical understanding of why the promise philosophy is so important and how anyone can use it to enhance the lives of his or her customers, associates (employees), influencers, and, for that matter, organization stakeholders.

A wide variety of examples and profiles have been utilized to illustrate how the BrandPromise concepts and methodology can apply to individuals, traditional corporate and product brands, professional service firms, charitable and philanthropic organizations, and member-centric businesses and associations. Brand profiles include genuine brands that are worldwide, such as Ketel One, Tourism Vancouver, the Make-A-Wish Foundation, Destination Marketing Association International, Costco, ANNIKA (Annika Sorenstam), and Callison Architecture, as well as SAFE Credit Union, RK Dixon, and Bartell Hotels, which enjoy significant success in their respective markets. Regardless of the organization or the situation, everyone wants a promise.

The search for substance in competitive strategic thinking has moved from advertising to marketing to branding, and more recently to "promise." Many leading businesses and intellectual thought leaders are beginning to talk about the importance of a commitment to a promise in all types of organizations. A *Harvard Business Review* article titled "What High-Tech Managers Need to Know about Brands" refers to this new way of thinking as, "A sea of change in managerial attitudes from a product-centric to a promise-centric business model."[1]

All too often, the hype of a new medical breakthrough, the fanfare of the next largest corporate merger or acquisition, or the next new technology has proven to be a disappointment to customers, associates, and shareholders, thereby resulting in broken promises.

The promise philosophy separates substance from hype and provides a practical guide for any organization or individual on how to make the right promise and how to keep it. Making a real promise to customers, associates, and shareholders is a basic moral issue—it's the right thing to do, and it's the right way to build success.

Every organization should be asking and answering the question, "What's our promise?"

WHAT IS A PROMISE?

A *promise* is something you can count on, an assurance, a commitment that something will happen. It's also meant to be used in a positive sense as the *Random House Webster's Unabridged Dictionary* states, it's an "indication of future excellence or achievement."

In our use throughout the book, a promise commitment is intended to communicate a genuine and positive expectation of distinctive functional and emotional benefits. It's the basis for a Genuine Brand. The promise concept revolves around the importance of focusing on how a brand wants its customers, associates, influencers, and, for that matter, all of its stakeholders to feel. It is this paradigm shift that provides the kind of success that truly admired brands enjoy.

THE RIGHT BRANDPROMISE

The right BrandPromise rests on three principles:

1. Provide a unique experience with products and services that enhance customers' lives.
2. Achieve associate (employee) partnership, passion, and support for a promise.
3. Create a perception of exceptional value and distinctive benefits.

These principles serve as an organization's "reality check" and enable it to evaluate whether or not a proposed promise will produce the desired brand experience.

CHAPTER OUTLINE

- Chapter 1 outlines the required organizational mindset that's necessary for a product to become a genuine brand.

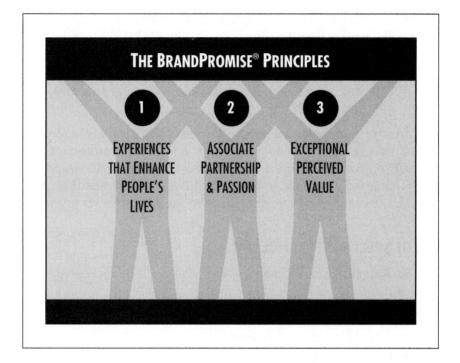

- Chapter 2 introduces the PromiseRule which defines how customers should be treated.
- Chapter 3 details the process for developing an organization's promise. Doing a good job is not enough; it's all about how your customers feel.
- Chapter 4 identifies the secrets for delivering a successful promise and explains the important role an organization's associates play in delivering the successful promise.
- Chapter 5 addresses the five ways that organizations can keep their promises and avoid broken promises.
- Chapter 6 reveals the methodology for predicting brand success.
- Chapter 7 provides the framework for creating community brands and introduces the destination BrandScience process with a detailed look at how to do it.
- Chapter 8 is the roadmap to follow to develop a strategy for a personal brand with professional insights from celebrities.

- Chapter 9 focuses on specialized promise applications for member-centric businesses, charitable and philanthropic organizations, professional service firms, and associations.
- Chapter 10 reviews the detailed process for building genuine brands.

At the conclusion of most chapters, we profile a genuine brand that we believe demonstrates an understanding of the BrandPromise philosophy, which provides valuable insights. Each chapter also has a thought guide, which outlines key thoughts to remember as you are developing your own promise.

USE OF SPECIFIC TERMINOLOGY

Please note that the following words are used to represent specific concepts to make the book more enjoyable.

- BrandPromise   *promise*
- BrandMindset   *mindset*
- Brand Blueprint   *blueprint*

Following the Acknowledgments, we have provided a "Brandictionary" that explains the terms listed above as well as a variety of other brand and promise-related terms and definitions to assist in understanding the concepts behind the BrandPromise. Please take a few minutes to review them before you read the book. Additionally, every organization should consider developing a Brandictionary guide that outlines the correct "brand-speak" for all associates related to their promise.

We have included a brand index, which lists many of the brands used as examples throughout this book. You can find that listing as well as their Web site address or URL addresses at the end of the book. You can also access this information at www.brandpromise.com.

I sincerely wish you the best of success as you make a promise.

Duane E. Knapp

ACKNOWLEDGMENTS

From my earliest memories, I have always admired people who demonstrate the "power of a promise" in all aspects of their daily lives. For the following people, the basic concept of a promise is deeply embedded in their character. I am thankful every day for the unique opportunity of having been positively influenced by many wonderful people who have provided me with the "promise" point of view.

The opportunity to learn from Michael Gehrisch, chief executive officer of the Destination Marketing Association International, and other travel and hospitality leaders at many convention and visitors bureaus (CVBs) including Bill Talbert of the Miami CVB; Spurgeon Richardson of the Atlanta CVB; Bill Peepers, formerly of the Orlando CVB; Rick Antonson, Walt Judas, and Sarah Kirby of Tourism Vancouver; Melissa McLean of Tourism Victoria; Mark Lieberman of L.A., Inc.; Reint Reinders and Kevin Kane of the Memphis CVB; Misti Kerns of the Santa Monica CVB; Debbie Lee of Santa Monica's Bayside District; Beth Carmichael and David Turgeon of the Napa Valley CVB; Leon Maisel of the Mobile Bay CVB; Dan O'Byrne of Little Rock CVB; Doug Neilson and Mary Denis of Visit Milwaukee; Jim Luttjohann of the Ventura Visitors and Convention Bureau; Maura Gast of the Irving CVB; Spurgeon Richardson of the Atlanta CVB; and Jon Hutchinson of the Sydney CVB has been a privilege.

Special thanks to each of the exceptional professionals and executives who have provided me with their valuable expertise, including Richard Bartell, Dana Irby, and Bobbi Brieske of Bartell Hotels; Dale Henley, Jeff Wood, Becky Skaggs, and Scott Smith of Haggen Food & Pharmacy and TOP Food and Drug; Mark Steinberg of IMG; Annika Sorenstam; Mike McGee and Kristin Moye of ANNIKA, Inc.; Charlie Mechem, commissioner emeritus of the LPGA; Dan Dutton of Stimson Lumber; Bill Bishop; Rachel Schoenewald of AutoSport; Irv Sandman and Bob Cumbow of Graham & Dunn; Sheila Fox of Fox Marketing Network; Warren Bryant and Mark Holz of Longs Drugs; Robin Wiegerink and Jessica Factor of the American Society of Echocardiography; Carl Van Fleet and Jill Hott of In-N-Out;

Craig Bachman of Lane Powell; Jeff Hendricks of Alaska Ocean Seafood; Tim Lewis of Corporate Air; Dr. Bijoy Khanderia and Dale Rustad of the Mayo Clinic; Harry Levitt of MullinTBG; Tom Waldron of Waldron & Company; Kevin Foster-Keddie and Dennis Karras of Washington State Employees Credit Union; John Fenton and David Snodgrass of Affinity Federal Credit Union; Steve Stoddard of Restaurants Unlimited, Inc.; and Michael Donahue.

The *BrandPromise* book would not have been possible without the insights and assistance of the Nolet family; Bill Eldien and Vinutha James of Ketel One; Jim Sinegal and Dana Sullivan of Costco; David Williams, Lindsey Harris, and Michael Pressendo of the Make-A-Wish Foundation; Greg Norman and Brian Stevens of Great White Shark Enterprises; Craig and Kathryn Hall and Mike Reynolds of Hall Wines; Henry Wirz of SAFE Credit Union; Bill Karst of Callison; Bob and Bryan Dixon and Sue Hill of RK Dixon; Bruce Blomgren of Dyson & Dyson; James Turner of JT's Bar-B-Que; Avril Weisman of Community Action Partnership; and Tony Simons of Cornell University.

I appreciate the many talented professionals who have shared their thoughts and words, including Kathy Fredell, Bonnie Durrance, Don Morgan, Andy Levine, James Clark, and Blaine Becker.

My heartfelt thanks to Orin Smith for his excellent foreword, Mary Glenn and Jane Palmieri of McGraw-Hill, Roberta Mantus for her exceptional editing, and to Dana Kirschbaum-Rodriguez of BrandStrategy, Inc., for her significant editorial contribution, dedication, and professional friendship.

BRANDICTIONARY®
Definitions to Help You Deliver a BrandPromise Commitment

It's important for organizations that make a BrandPromise commitment to create a Brandictionary guide outlining specific terminology and definitions that they use. It is crucial that everyone in an organization use the same vocabulary, such as how to refer to its customers. For example, Target and In-N-Out refer to customers as "guests," and Disneyland identifies employees as "cast members."

Throughout this book, we have used a variety of promise and brand-related terminology, our own definitions, and other terms that are indicated by their source. We thought it might be helpful to identify these for your convenience as you read the book.

BrandPromise®, BrandMindset®, Brandictionary®, BrandScience™, BrandPsychic™, and BrandStrategy™ are trademarks of BrandStrategy, Inc. All other trademarks are the property of their respective owners. In addition, other easily recognizable brands and brand names are used for illustrative purposes and are not associated with BrandStrategy, Inc.

Brand Assessment: An objective analysis of a brand's image and perception.

Brand Balance: A brand's balance between emotional attributes and functional reality.

Brand Blueprint: (1) The disciplined action and process required to create, design, and build a brand communications plan. (2) The character and structure of a brand's representations; that is, the architecture of a brand (brand name, byline, tag line, BrandPromise, and graphic representation).

Brand Culturalization: (1) The engaging of all associates (employees) in the sum total of beliefs, behaviors, and characteristics of a particular brand. (2) The act of raising the level of awareness with a view toward improvement (self and organizational). (3) The act of living a brand's promise.

BrandMindset®: The ability to think like a genuine brand.

Brand Paradigm Shift: (1) A fundamental change in the strategic model for a business or industry. (2) A significant change in a brand's perceived distinctiveness.

BrandPromise®: The essence (heart, soul, and spirit) of the functional and emotional benefits that customers and influencers receive when experiencing a brand's products and services.

BrandPsychic™: The ability to interpret and identify a brand's future trend.

BrandScience™: The study of the relationship between brands and their stakeholders' functional and emotional perceptions.

Brand Stakeholders:

Associates: Employees, agents, representatives, or anyone who acts on behalf of the brand.

Customers: Current, prospective, and past customers, clients, patients, and so on.

Consumers: The general public or a specific target audience.

Influencers: People who influence others' opinions and perceptions of a brand.

BrandStrategy™ Doctrine: The comprehensive action plan (roadmap) used by an organization to define its essence (the BrandPromise), the purpose of which is to create a paradigm shift and a "position of privilege" (sustainable competitive advantage) and to optimize overall brand equity.

Brand Transformation: Changing an organization's form, appearance, nature, or character to enhance customer experiences.

Brand Visualization: An understanding of where associates, customers, consumers, and influencers envision a brand to be in the future.

Community Brand: The internalized sum of a community's impressions in the minds of visitors, residents, business owners, investors, developers, community leaders, and so on.

Customer Bill of Rights: A commitment to fulfill specific customer expectations.

Customer Recovery: The restoration and enhancement of a brand's relationship with customers.

Destination Promise: The strategic mindset that creates a unique destination in the minds of guests, influencers, and stakeholders.

Distinctive: A positive connotation: unique, superior, worthy of special recognition, distinguished from others.

Emotional Tipping: The act of thanking or showing appreciation to someone without a material gift.

Genuine: Authentic, real, and trusted.

Genuine Brand: The internalized sum of all impressions received by consumers, customers, associates, and influencers resulting in a distinctive position in their mind's eye based on perceived emotional and functional benefits.

Higher Motives: Appealing to people's feelings related to goodness, trust, mercy, happiness, and so on.

Member-Centric: Relating to an organization that focuses its promise on enhancing its members' perception, image, and success.

Perceived Value: Customers' and consumers' perceptions based on their experience with a brand, including their time involved in a transaction, how they feel, and financial cost.

Personal Brand: The internalized sum of all impressions received by a person's "public" including friends, family, associates, and influencers.

Placeholder: An associate (employee) who does not deliver a promise.

Promise-Centric: Relating to a situation in which an organization's promise drives everything it does.

PromiseRule: Rule stating that people be treated better than they expect.

CHAPTER 1

The BrandMindset Philosophy

Take care of your reputation. It's your most valuable asset.
—The Complete Life's Little Instruction Book

THINKING LIKE A GENUINE BRAND

Brands are an asset. They should be created, developed, and managed with great care and due diligence. Having an overall process to create a successful strategy for a brand is essential to achieving long-term positive performance. My first book, *The BrandMindset*, laid the groundwork for creating and building genuine brands. Our process for building genuine brands is a science and not an art. It is outlined in Figure 1.1. A detailed outline of the process for creating genuine brands is provided in Chapter 10, Promise Perspectives, for your convenience.

Let's examine what it means to think like a genuine brand. Genuine brands clearly follow a strategy so that they will be perceived as distinctive from other choices, more relevant to their customers, consumers, associates, and influencers; and they offer superior perceived value.

Throughout this book we use the terms *customers, consumers, associates,* and *influencers* as outlined in Figure 1.2 to identify an organization's stakeholders. For our purposes shareholders are included in influencers.

1

FIGURE 1.1

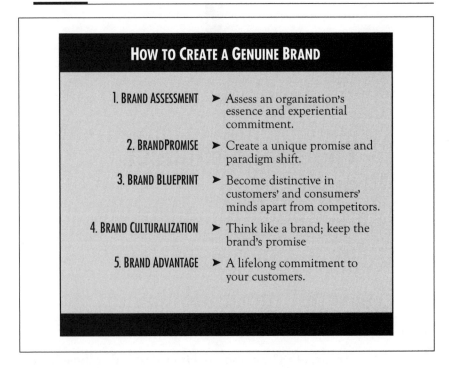

FIGURE 1.2

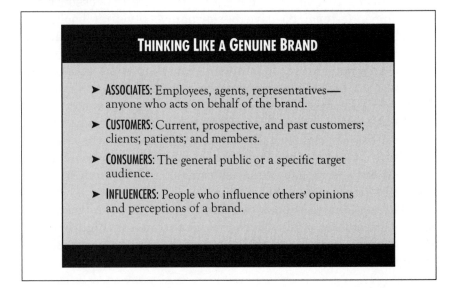

To become a one of a kind brand, an organization must think like a "genuine brand," and this requires a different mindset, perspective, and strategy from business as usual. Successful organizations need to be perceived as distinctive and make a BrandPromise commitment (promise) to their customers and consumers that delivers emotional and functional benefits.

When an organization thinks and acts like a Genuine Brand, the entire organization understands what the promise is all about and how to deliver the right experience. Everyone from the CEO to the frontline associate has the same mindset. Successful implementation of a promise initiative requires that everyone in the organization be onboard. It's not optional!

Leading brands that deliver on their promise will benefit from enhanced customer satisfaction and profitable pricing opportunities as well as increased pride and the power of a positive experience. The key to becoming a successful Genuine Brand is to focus on providing distinctive and relevant experiences for customers that provide lasting and memorable positive impressions.

Genuine brands make a promise, and they deliver on that promise consistently, eagerly, and at their customer's convenience. The power of a promise is based on what customers say about a brand to their friends and their feelings toward the brand. In a word association exercise, when consumers are asked, "What is a brand?" the most frequent response is: a name. Consumers see brand names every day; they are bombarded with thousands of brand impressions in print and across all forms of electronic media. It's impossible to escape them. Don't get me wrong. Having a good brand name is important and offers several advantages. However, there is much more to a strategy for a brand than a name.

Successful brands lead the way. They become their promise, and they behave like a guarantee. Yet brands really exist only in people's minds. Brands tell customers whether something will make them feel better or make their life easier, better, solve a problem, or fulfill a need or desire.

The *Random House Dictionary of the English Language* defines a brand as: "A kind or variety of something distinguished by some distinctive characteristic." It is the *distinctive traits* that separate brands from commodity items in consumers'

FIGURE 1.3

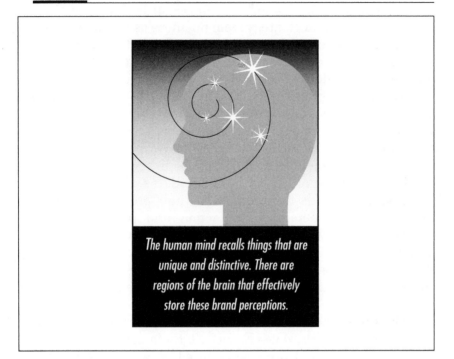

The human mind recalls things that are unique and distinctive. There are regions of the brain that effectively store these brand perceptions.

minds. What do people remember? Human memory researchers have found that the mind remembers things that are unique and distinctive. The goal is to be perceived as unique and distinctive and not be just one of many in a sea of sameness.

If you think genuine brands are primarily the result of marketing departments and advertising messages, think again. People process literally thousands of bits of information throughout the course of a day including advertising and marketing impressions. The ones that rise above the clutter and stick in the mind affect decision making. The truly influential ones connect with consumers on a meaningful and emotional level; that is to say, they genuinely fulfill a need or want and a desired feeling. These are genuine brands.

A *genuine brand* is defined as: "The internalized sum of all impressions received by customers and consumers resulting in a distinctive position in their mind's eye based on perceived emotional and functional benefits." *Distinctive* is the key word to understanding the real meaning of a brand. It's not an organization or company that gets to decide whether or not its brand is distinctive. A brand is distinctive only if its customers, consumers, associates, and influencers perceive and believe that it truly is.

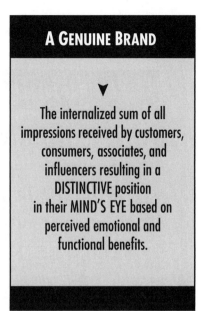

A GENUINE BRAND

▼

The internalized sum of all impressions received by customers, consumers, associates, and influencers resulting in a DISTINCTIVE position in their MIND'S EYE based on perceived emotional and functional benefits.

GENUINE BRAND EXPECTATIONS

In order for an organization to become a *genuine brand*, several expectations must be met:

1. Is it truly distinctive or different in a manner that is important and valued by its customers?
2. Is it committed to providing certain emotional and functional benefits for its customers?
3. Does it consistently fulfill its promise and deliver on its commitments?

Genuine brands exist *only* to add value. They understand that people make real-life decisions every day on both an emotional and a functional level. Genuine brands promise that, "We'll make you feel great about your experience." Then they deliver on that promise. Genuine brands treat people right and exceed expectations. The BrandPromise methodology is described in Figure 1.4, and each step in the process is explained in detail in the following chapters.

Genuine brands overcome adversity more easily than average brands. They make people feel better before, during, and after the experience. For example, think about the last time you made a call to a customer service department.Was it a pleasant experience? Were you able to talk with a "live" person immediately? Or, as happens with most organizations, were you placed on hold for minutes or even hours or waited days for a response?

FIGURE 1.4

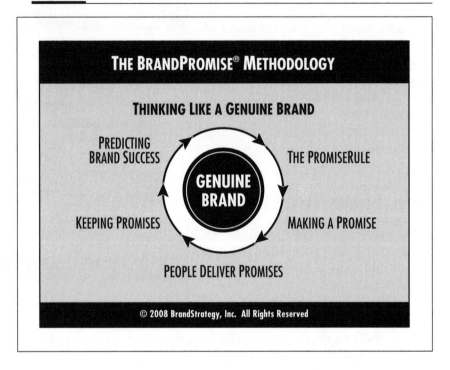

A business executive told me his most recent customer *dis-service* experience. The hard drive on his computer crashed. Knowing it was still on warranty, he called the manufacturer's customer service number (a major e-commerce computer company). After waiting on hold for over an hour and a half, he was told by the customer service representative that he called the wrong department (since when is customer service the wrong department?). The customer service representative gave him a different number to call and wouldn't even transfer him. This call, to technical support, resulted in another two-hour wait. After a total of over six hours on hold and less than thirty minutes of actual talk-time with real people (half of which was spent receiving a wrong diagnosis and bad information), it was determined that the hard drive was indeed bad and that a replacement drive would be shipped. Adding insult to injury, the replacement hard drive turned out to be worse than the original and needed to be replaced, resulting in more phones calls and more hold time. This e-commerce manufacturer even invoiced the customer for the warranty replacement part in the event that the worthless drive wasn't returned within a specified time frame.

TRAINING BEFORE ADVERTISING

▼

For years, Starbucks spent more money on training than on advertising.

If this company had been "thinking like a Genuine Brand," this bad experience would have been avoided.

For a brand to be noticed and eventually chosen, it must be effective at communicating its unique attributes in a wide variety of applications. Building a successful brand can be done without an extensive or expensive advertising campaign. Great brands, such as Starbucks, were not built on advertising; they were built around a promise.

When a brand's products and services have been significantly distinguished, public relations and other third-party endorsements can be effective tools for building genuine brands. They cost less than traditional advertising, and they offer a higher degree of credibility.

Perceived quality is an essential brand ingredient. There are many organizations and associations (Baldrige Awards, J.D. Power, AAA, Consumer Reports, etc.) that rate quality. However, the rating system that matters most is the one customers and prospective customers use in their mind's eye.

Satisfied customers are important. However a brand's best marketing strategy is delighted customers! Delighted consumers become the brand's primary influencers and most loyal customers.

There are varying degrees of loyalty, ranging from the dissatisfied to the loyal. Dissatisfied customers are always on the lookout for something better. They shop around. Satisfied customers may or may not purchase again. They are content, but their loyalty to one brand may be suspect.

On the other hand, loyal or delighted customers are committed to future purchases with the organization's brand. When organizations' brands exceed customer expectations, the "wow" experience occurs. What's the "wow" about? It is when customers, consumers, members, constituents, clients, and the public consider the brand to be a "friend."

Rewarding loyalty can be a wonderful strategy. When it becomes the sole reason for customers returning, it can become something else, something I refer to as *brand bribery*. Brand bribery lurks in commodity-driven industries characterized by a discernible lack of differentiated products or outstanding service.

THE TRUST FACTOR

We use the word "genuine" because it means authentic, and something that's genuine is supposed to be real and trusted. At the core of a *genuine brand* is the feeling of trust. The importance of trust cannot be overstated. Organizations that believe in creating genuine brands are able to benefit from the "integrity dividend," as Cornell Professor Tony Simons calls it. Tony surveyed 100 successful executives for his new book, *The Integrity Dividend* (to be published by Jossey-Bass in 2008), to investigate how behavior integrity works.

This executive survey, along with Tony's earlier research,

> Showed that associate perceptions of managers' behavioral integrity—the extent to which they kept promises and lived by their professed values—had strong bottom-line consequences. The executives I spoke with agreed with that conclusion. However, they suggested that the ways in which this principle enhances performances go well beyond just the financial returns.[1]

Tony concluded that,

> Behavioral integrity forms a foundation for trust and interpersonal warmth and loyalty. It builds credibility and leads to a personal reputation. By creating predictability, it enables others to predict your judgments and to act on reliable, accurate information. It all but eliminates the need for associates to wonder and discuss what your agenda is and whether you mean what you say. These immediate consequences of integrity echo far beyond the attitudes and behaviors of associates and directly impact the customer's experience.[2]

FIGURE 1.5

THE TRUST FACTOR

"You gain a huge advantage when people know your word is as good as gold. In today's world, there seem to be fewer and fewer promises we can fully count on. And people really appreciate it when yours is one of them. You lose some tactical flexibility by keeping your word—but you earn a dividend as well."

—Tony Simons

Used with permission.

Tony ran a survey of over 6,000 associates at over 70 Holiday Inn Hotels and so demonstrated the impact of perceived managerial integrity on dollar profits. A mere 1/8 point difference between hotels on the five-point scale means a difference of roughly $250,000 profit per year. Many of the hotels with high management integrity converted over 10 percent more of each revenue dollar into profits than others.

Does behavioral integrity make a difference to the bottom line? Tony says, "Emphatically, yes. A huge yes. I had stalked and found the integrity dividend."

Where associates reported high integrity on the part of their managers, the results were impressive:

- Deeper associate commitment
- Lower associate turnover
- Superior customer service
- Higher profitability

Enlightened leaders are becoming more aware of the importance of the trust factor across all of an organization's key audiences; customers, consumers, associates, and influencers. Airlines provide a perfect laboratory for this thesis.

Any commercial airline flight could provide an example of the importance of trust and its relationship to passengers' experiences. The level of satisfaction and trust among an airline's gate agents, pilots, flight attendants, and ground crews is reflected in the way they feel and the experience they provide to their passengers.

Let's examine a typical experience for a passenger. Whether it's the gate agent or a flight attendant, the first clue is the body language including their facial expressions and the greeting. These three factors can predict, with some assurance, the type of experience you're going to "enjoy" as a passenger. The actual interaction between you and an airline's associates will then determine how you actually feel. The point of the trust factor is that the associate's attitude and behavior toward each passenger will be significantly influenced by the employee's perception of the trust factor within his or her organization.

This is not meant as a criticism of any airline employees, but rather it is intended to reflect the reality of the fact that an organization's mental environment directly affects the customer experience.

As an example, Colleen Barrett, president of Southwest Airlines says, "What we are looking for are people who care, are very other-oriented rather than 'I.' We're looking for people who take the business seriously, but not themselves. A sense of humor is a must. And we look for people who were raised on values like the golden rule."[3]

She further explains, "We're a very forgiving company in terms of good honest mistakes, but we're not at all forgiving about attitude and behavior and demeanor."[4]

THE PROMISE IS THE FOUNDATION OF A BRAND'S EXPERIENCE

The right promise is fundamental to becoming a genuine brand and delivering a distinctive experience. There are three principles to achieving the right promise for everyone involved in a brand (customers, consumers, associates, and influencers). (See Figure 1.6.)

1. Provide a unique experience with products and services that enhance customers' lives.
2. Achieve associate partnership, passion, and support for a promise.
3. Create a perception of exceptional value and distinctive benefits.

FIGURE 1.6

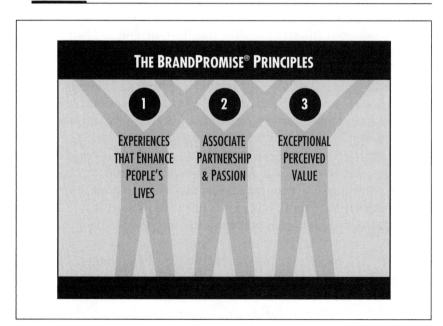

THE BRANDPROMISE® PRINCIPLES

1 — EXPERIENCES THAT ENHANCE PEOPLE'S LIVES

2 — ASSOCIATE PARTNERSHIP & PASSION

3 — EXCEPTIONAL PERCEIVED VALUE

BRANDING

▼

Branding is usually about messages and images and not the ALL ENCOMPASSING experience.

As you can see, creating the right promise is not just about an advertising message or a new logo. It's much more than any of these. When asked if a company or an organization has a promise, executives frequently say: "Yes, we have a branding initiative," or "We've gone through a whole branding exercise."

What we are talking about is creating a promise, not about branding. This is not to say that branding for some organizations has not included a promise.

Most of the time branding means a new message, image, or promotional campaign and not a comprehensive commitment to the entire experience that a brand provides customers, consumers, associates, and influencers internally and externally.

All too often branding becomes focused on hype and not substance, or worse it gets lost between various silos or departments within an organization. Rob Rush's insights in his article titled "Top of Mind: Let's 'Operationalize' the Brand Promise" at BrandWeek.com illustrates this familiar problem. He presents an example of a typical executive dialogue for a branding situation. "What our firm is lacking is the ability to 'operationalize' our brand … what's missing is the internal agreement on the brand experience and how to deliver it. The level of dissonance is invisible to the customer, but makes it virtually impossible to satisfy them."[5]

Rush's article demonstrates the typical real-world challenges related to branding. Any and every branding or brand initiative, campaign, or program must answer the question: is this about "substance"; that is, is this a promise, or is it "hype"? If the answer is substance, then you're ready to enhance people's lives.

ENHANCING CUSTOMERS' LIVES

The first question we think about with potential clients is whether they are sincerely interested in enhancing their customers' lives.

This may sound utopian; however, it's the way we think. In fact, we believe that the difference between genuine brands and all the other businesses is that genuine brands are determined to enhance their customers' lives.

A popular notion is that if you want to understand your customers' needs, you need to walk in their shoes. There is no question that this makes sense, but what does "walking in their shoes" really mean? It means having a real experience complete with the emotional and functional perspective of a real customer.

Here's an example: Talk about walking in someone's shoes! Dr. Scott Dye of San Francisco Sports Medicine and Orthopaedic illustrates the idea. According to *Runner's World* magazine, Dr. Dye wanted to really understand the source of pain related to knee degeneration and injury, specifically, what is known as patellofemoral pain syndrome (PFPS), a very frequent occurrence.

He decided that the only way to truly know the source of knee pain related to PFPS was to have his healthy knee surgically probed without anesthesia. "He felt only slight discomfort as it touched his ACL and articular cartilage, however, when the probe touched the synovium tissue at the base of his knee cap, the study quickly turned medieval." A light touch to the synovium, Dr. Dye learned, can cause sharp pain, "eliciting involuntary vocalizations."[6] Understanding the source of this type of knee pain is all about enhancing patients' lives and providing important medical science advancements.

Your job may not require the personal sacrifice and pain that Dr. Dye endured to understand how to enhance his patients' lives, however, your responsibility to your customers is the same.

If you are in charge of a telephone call center or a customer service operation, the most important thing you can do is listen to a random sampling of calls and interactions every day. The purpose is not just to see if people are doing their job; but, more importantly, do they understand how your customers feel emotionally about their experience? Are you really willing to experience what your customers, consumers, and influencers feel when they interact with your brand?

Whether a brand is making diet pills or laptops, serving lunch or delivering packages, the critical question is, how is the brand enhancing its customers' lives today? Here are some questions to ask:

1. Do you use your products and services as much as your best customers do?
2. Do your customers talk positively about your brand to their friends as though they owned it?
3. Do you hire associates who have the emotional ability to make your customers feel special?
4. Does every associate really care about how his or her customers feel?
5. Do you have prospective associates waiting in line to join your organization or company?
6. Do your customers create their own positive descriptors for your brand such as the "Costco run" or Tar-shay for Target "style"? Do they tattoo your brand on their bodies like Harley-Davidson customers?
7. Do you treat customers better than you want to be treated?
8. Do you provide a no-hassle, nonconfrontational, unconditional guarantee of satisfaction?
9. Would you force your mother to navigate an automated phone system when she calls you?
10. Do you have a promise that every associate knows and believes in?

PASSIONATE ASSOCIATES

It seems to make perfect sense—having associates working in an organization who are truly passionate about what they are doing and are focused on customers' feelings. I constantly hear executives and managers saying, "It's so hard to find good people." In fact, I recall a conversation with executives at a very well-known brand in California explaining the difficulty of finding entry level associates.

I'm always pleasantly surprised to be greeted by a happy person at each In-N-Out restaurant in California or Nevada that I have visited. I marvel at their spotless restrooms, and even when I brought 20 international executives to an In-N-Out for lunch, their frontline associates made me feel great. So how can In-N-Out provide a positive experience every time and other organizations seem to struggle in their attempt to hire passionate associates? The answer: it's all about your expectations.

Restaurants Unlimited, Inc., employed the philosophy that its restaurant managers should always maintain a ready resource of talented potential associates to hire. Its restaurant managers are constantly out in their respective trade areas looking for people with exceptional attitudes at hotels, nearby malls, dry cleaners, other restaurants, and so on. The strategy was always to have a supply of possible new hires that had already passed the "attitude" test.

This philosophy is alive and well today at Restaurants Unlimited, which was founded in 1969 and operates many successful brands including, Palomino, Kincaid's, Stanford's, Newport Grill, Pizzeria Fondi, and others.

"We feel that a company has the responsibility to create a great place to work in order to accomplish exceptional results, and that means you have to hire the best and care about them," says Steve Stoddard, president and chief executive officer. Restaurants Unlimited's values have stood the test of time and are illustrated in Figure 1.7. The company's promise is reflected in its values.

We've all heard the adage, "Hire for attitude." You can teach them the job; however, this strategy takes it out of the traditional interview mode and into the real world. If you can observe people with passion in their current job, it's a much better predictor of how they will make your customers feel. We have all experienced an interview with a prospective associate only to have that person turn into an evil twin after he or she is hired.

Randy White, a private banking vice president for a large bank, understands the concept of being passionate. His reputation for service is remarkable, and he really acts as an advocate for his clients. He says, "You can pay someone to show up or to perform a certain number of tasks. However, you can't pay someone to care. If someone cares, it's all about who they are as a person." This is the real essence of what we are describing as passionate associates—people who are sincerely interested in creating exceptional experiences for others.

FIGURE 1.7

RESTAURANTS
UNLIMITED

We act GUEST FIRST.

We deliver high quality food &
beverage every time, at
reasonable prices.

We give great service and engage
each GUEST.

We hire the best and care
about them.

We are clean.

Used with permission.

Another perspective on passionate associates has to do with the "experience" mindset. Rick Hendrie believes, "Your Experience Is the Brand." In his article at www.hotel-online.com, he recommends, "As you consider your strategic direction, ask yourself a simple question, is it an experience I would pay to see again?"[7] Although his comments are directed at the hospitality industry, I feel that every transaction for every associate in every organization should be held to the "experience" test.

We explore in much more detail the "passionate people" aspects of delivering an organization's promise in Chapter 4.

ASSOCIATE PARTNERSHIP

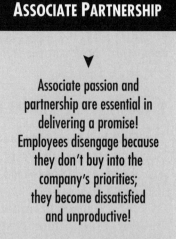

ASSOCIATE PARTNERSHIP

▼

Associate passion and partnership are essential in delivering a promise! Employees disengage because they don't buy into the company's priorities; they become dissatisfied and unproductive!

The saying goes, "People will support what they have helped to create." This couldn't be more important today. In our age of technology and digital communications, one would think that communications within organizations would be improved. However, it seems that associate involvement in critical strategic decisions is declining.

A recent *Harvard Business Review* article titled, "Promise Based Management" points out that "execution fails for a variety of depressingly familiar reasons."[8]

My observations conclude that more often than not associates don't even know about an organization's priorities, let alone buy into them. Developing a real and genuine partnership with associates across an organization's activities is management's responsibility. It's not just about communicating the priorities and the promise; it's about understanding what they really mean to the associates and how the associates translate the promise into a specific experience for customers.

In a 2007 survey of retail managers and senior executives, we asked them how much time they spent providing positive experiences for their associates and customers. Responses ranged from between 10 and 20 percent. Obviously, this was a real challenge. Building a meaningful partnership with associates requires a commitment upwards of 50 percent of managers' and executives' time to create the right environment for success.

Our work with clients has clearly demonstrated that associates need to feel that they have been involved in an organization's strategy, especially when it changes. Based on our experience, the results of associates' participation in the strategic process have proven to be extremely beneficial in every way.

If associates participate in the development of an organization's promise and its strategic priorities, then they may feel more motivated to take responsibility for delivering on the promise. However, it's critical that the right kind of employee is hired in the first place. We discuss this concept of a "partnership" with associates in Chapter 4.

CREATING EXCEPTIONAL PERCEIVED VALUE

Perceived value is at the crux of everyone's perception of his or her experience with any organization. All too often, companies are singularly possessed about the price of their products and services.

While price is important, it's only one part of three fundamental perceptions used to determine whether customers believe that what they are buying is worth the price. It's very important to exceed customer's emotional expectations and time-related expectations.

Customers develop their perception of value through a subjective feeling as a result of comparing the brand's product and service offerings with those of its competitors based on their own needs, preferences, buying behavior, and characteristics. Thus, a customer's perception of value constantly changes. Consequently, the brand's ability to deliver value and delight customers is deeply rooted in the promise.

Genuine brands create delighted customers who believe and trust the brand's ability to deliver value and are willing to pay an amount greater than the total cost of the products and services. Profits serve as one measure of how well a brand is creating delighted customers. However, long-term profit is more important than a strategy that increases profits in the short term at the expense of future brand equity.

In some cases, customers may perceive value to mean "lowest price." Lowest price is also translated to mean frequent sales and promotional discounts. A marketing position of "lowest price" is the most difficult to sustain and generally is an indication that

FIGURE 1.8

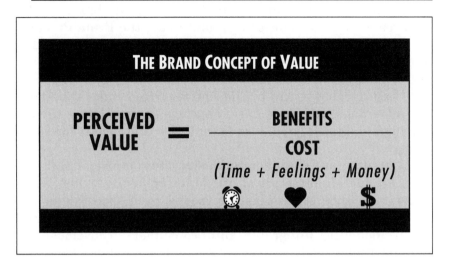

the brand or organization has become a commodity in the minds of consumers. The only distinctive point of difference that commodities have is usually price.

Genuine brands understand that a lowest-price strategy does not necessarily guarantee customer loyalty. Customers looking for the lowest price will primarily be loyal to the price, not the brand. On the other hand, when customers perceive that a brand consistently delivers value, the brand has established the foundation to become a genuine brand. As a result, genuine brands enjoy higher degrees of profitability, customer loyalty, and enhanced brand equity.

When an organization is "thinking like a brand," everyone understands that customers are buying more than just products or services. Genuine brands never focus solely on a product alone; they are committed to their brand as a product and service. To refer to a product alone is to say that the customer doesn't care about time, convenience, feelings, and overall satisfaction. In the Brand Value formula, the perceived benefits should exceed the total cost. The ability to deliver positive perceived value is determined by consumers' perceptions of a brand's benefits versus its total cost (functional and emotional).

Any successful brand must be good at its business, that is, "doing things right." However, building optimum brand equity requires "doing the right things" and living the BrandPromise. Genuine brands that dominate their segments always own a distinctive position in the consumer's mind and habitually create positive paradigm shifts that consumers enjoy. Figure 1.8 lists time first because it can be the source of tremendous competitive advantage. Everyone has a shortage of time, hence time is extremely valuable, and it is becoming a significant driver of perceived value.

Genuine brands understand that their products and services are not simply a set of attributes or just a "thing." They understand that consumers are moved by the gestalt of the brand—all its tangible and intangible (functional and emotional) benefits, integrated into consumers' consciousness. Genuine brands deliver a distinctive promise that creates memorable value reaching far beyond their customer base.

Any company or organization that wants to be a genuine brand must focus on its promise to its customers, influencers, and employees. The widespread focus on "image" without the first requirement being a genuine promise is the real issue today, and I believe that this is one of the biggest challenges that traditional advertisers face.

A brand is only as good or as valuable as its promise. Imagine if every advertising agency required its clients to have a promise that their associates were delivering before creating any advertisement, promotion, or communication. Without a promise, a brand is at risk of failure.

The following Brand Profile of Ketel One Vodka serves up an excellent example of how to think like a *genuine brand* and keep the promise for over 300 years.

BRAND PROFILE

KETEL ONE VODKA

If Joannes Nolet, founder of the Nolet Distillery, knew back in 1691 that his recipes and techniques would still be used more than 300 years later to produce one of the finest ultrapremium vodkas, he probably wouldn't be surprised. His relentless passion to build a dynasty that would last for generations and his commitment to creating the perfect distillation process is showcased today in one of the world's finest handcrafted spirits—Ketel One Vodka.

In 1691, Joannes Nolet arrived in the city of Schiedam, Holland. It was the perfect city to open a distillery—grain was available at the local auction, horses and carts were readily available for cargo, the city was close to major ports, and boats were moored at the waterside. While perfecting the distillation process, Joannes noted his accomplishments in a journal, thus marking the establishment of the Nolet Distillery.

Joannes understood that the finest raw materials are imperative to the creation of vodka, which is why Ketel One Vodka is made exclusively from wheat. The craft of flawless distillation is supervised by a master distiller at the Nolet Distillery. Utilizing the original copper pot still "Distilleerketel #1," after

FIGURE 1.9

Used with permission.

which Ketel One Vodka is proudly named, the master distiller oversees the process step by step. As contents of the distillate are heated over a gentle, hand-stoked fire, the temperature and alcohol levels are regulated to ensure the best vodka possible. Only the core of each distillate meets the Nolet standards for smoothness, so the first and last 100 gallons are discarded for being either too harsh or too weak. Once distillation is complete, the vodka is filtered over loose charcoal and rests in tile-lined tanks until it's ready. Settling for nothing less than perfection, a member of the Nolet family always tastes each batch of vodka to approve its release and its right to bear the name Ketel One.

As the fame of Ketel One Vodka continues to grow, the Nolets are proud to provide consumers with smooth, great-tasting vodka. Current chairman and tenth-generation owner, Carl Nolet, Sr., believes the factors contributing to Ketel One Vodka's success are the focus on the superiority of the product, the distillation and raw materials utilized, and the positive word-of-mouth recommendations. These factors aid in consumers' identification with the brand's promise as follows.

FIGURE 1.10

THE ORIGINAL

DISTILLING KETEL Nº1

There is nothing like the pleasure of Ketel One. We invite our friends to enjoy our clean, crisp, velvety smooth genuine vodka. Since 1691, the Nolet family has been handcrafting the finest classic spirits using their authentic recipes.

The dedication of each Ketel One employee to bring the brand's *promise* to life includes the sharing of experiences and education that they call *discovery marketing.* Tours of the Nolet Distillery in Holland and the Carl Nolet, Sr., Hospitality Center at the U.S. headquarters give consumers a snapshot of how a unique product is made and how it is enjoyed. Discovery marketing is an unprecedented opportunity for consumers, bartenders, and business partners to learn about vodka and the history of Ketel One by participating in taste tests and the sharing of recipes. Through these experiences each group makes a connection with the brand. These experiences also encourage long-term loyalty, and they open the communication of their "new discovery" to others.

FIGURE 1.11

Spurred by the success of Ketel One Vodka, Ketel One Citroen was introduced. The Nolet's recipe for Ketel One Citroen was created from previous generations' experiences and expert knowledge of blending citrus flavors. Ketel One Citroen is an all-natural, citrus-flavored vodka that combines lemon and lime to achieve the perfect balance of fine spirit and natural citrus. It is handcrafted to the same exacting standards as Ketel One Vodka.

Like his ancestors, Carl, Sr., is passionate about the art of distilling and protects the family's secret recipes by keeping them locked in a vault at the distillery. By staying true to his family's traditions and techniques dating back to 1691, his company produces products that this Dutch heritage is proud of.

FIGURE 1.12

Just as nine generations before him, Carl, Sr., will someday pass on the techniques and recipes to his sons, Carl, Jr., and Bob Nolet. The eleventh-generation Nolets are becoming highly skilled experts in the world of distilling and are passionate about the family business. It is evident that three centuries of heritage and commitment to excellence are present in every sip of Ketel One Vodka.

THOUGHT GUIDE

THINKING LIKE A GENUINE BRAND

- Genuine brands clearly follow a strategy of being perceived as distinctive from other choices; as being more relevant to their customers, associates, and influencers; and they offer superior perceived value.
- Genuine brands make a promise, and they deliver on that promise consistently, eagerly, and at their customers' convenience.
- In order to be perceived as a genuine brand, an organization or individual brand must meet several expectations:
  - Is it truly distinctive in a manner that is important and valued by its customers?
  - Is it committed to providing certain emotional and functional benefits for its customers?
  - Does it consistently fulfill its promise and deliver on its commitments?
- There are many firms that rate various brands' product quality and service. However, the most important rating is the one in the minds of a brand's customers.
- Genuine brands gain a huge advantage because they can be trusted. Tony Simons calls this the "Integrity Dividend."
- The right promise:
  - Enhances people's lives
  - Achieves associate and partnership and passion
  - Creates a perception of exceptional value

- If you really want to understand your customers' needs, you must walk in their shoes.
- Is a brand really enhancing its customers' lives? Here are 10 key questions to consider:
  1. Do we use our products and services as much as our best customers?
  2. Do our customers talk positively about our brand to their friends as though they owned it?
  3. Do we hire associates who have the emotional capability to make our customers feel special?
  4. Does every associate really care about how his or her customers feel?
  5. Do we have prospective associates waiting in line to join our organization or company?
  6. Do our customers create their own positive descriptors for our brand such as the "Costco run," Tar-shay for Target "style," or tattoo your brand on their bodies like Harley-Davidson?
  7. Do we treat customers better than they expect to be treated?
  8. Do we provide a no-hassle, nonconfrontational, unconditional guarantee of satisfaction?
  9. Would I force my mother to navigate an automated phone system when she calls?
  10. Do we have a promise that every associate knows and believes in?
- The quality of a brand's relationship with its associates has a direct correlation with the brand's ability to deliver its promise.
- If associates participate in the development of an organization's promise, they will take responsibility for delivering the promise.
- Perceived value is the combination of customers' perspectives related to time, feelings, and money as they experience the benefits of a specific product or service.

CHAPTER 2

The PromiseRule: Enhancing People's Lives

So long as we love we serve; so long as we are loved by others,
I would almost say we are indispensable.
—Robert Louis Stevenson

SERVICE COMPARED TO A PROMISE

Recently, we have been conducting our promise "tests" on businesses that people complain about. Interestingly enough, we visited businesses that had disappointed customers and asked this question during our transaction. By the way, "What's your promise?" Not one of these businesses' employees understood the question, let alone could explain what their promise was.

We believe that there is a real opportunity to provide customers with a pleasant surprise. It's called the PromiseRule as indicated in Figure 2.1.

Danny Meyer, renowned New York restaurant owner, makes our point: "One of the real keys to success of our restaurants is understanding the difference between service and hospitality. Service is how well something is done technically, and hospitality is how good something feels emotionally."[1]

In 2006 Accenture, a global consulting firm, conducted an online survey of more than 1,000 consumers. "Fifty-seven percent of respondents said customer service technologies such as

FIGURE 2.1

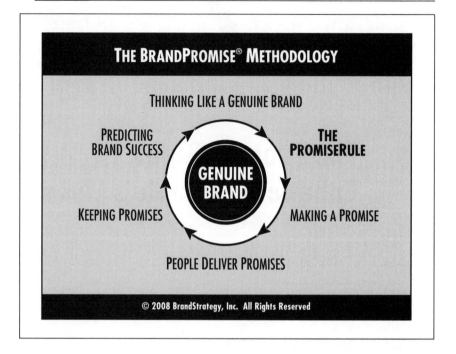

automated phone service and live online chat had not done anything to improve service levels. While nearly half (46 percent) of
respondents reported they quit doing business with a company
in at least one industry category in the past year as a result of
poor service, some industries fared worse than others. For
instance, retailers suffered the greatest number of customer
defections due to poor service."[2]

Service is probably the most misused term in business
today. It means nothing unless it is connected to how a company
wants its customers to feel.

How do you feel when you walk into a Starbucks compared
to a typical coffee shop? There is a feeling that connects the customer with the brand. It is the Starbucks' promise of the "third
place"—a place to relax, indulge, rejuvenate, and enjoy that distinguishes the Starbucks experience from others.

Let's examine a couple of examples of "business as usual."
(See Figure 2.2.)

FIGURE 2.2

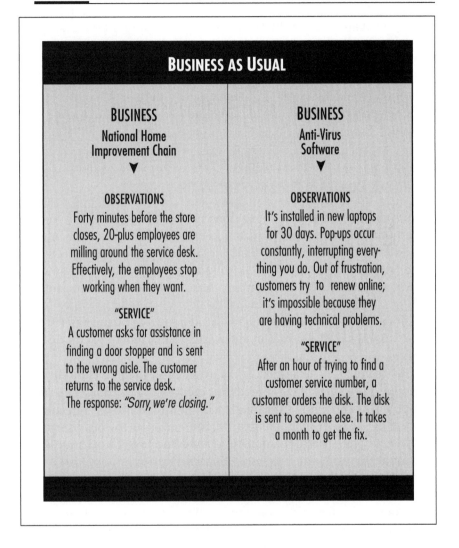

BUSINESS AS USUAL

BUSINESS
National Home
Improvement Chain
▼

OBSERVATIONS
Forty minutes before the store
closes, 20-plus employees are
milling around the service desk.
Effectively, the employees stop
working when they want.

"SERVICE"
A customer asks for assistance in
finding a door stopper and is sent
to the wrong aisle. The customer
returns to the service desk.
The response: *"Sorry, we're closing."*

BUSINESS
Anti-Virus
Software
▼

OBSERVATIONS
It's installed in new laptops
for 30 days. Pop-ups occur
constantly, interrupting everything you do. Out of frustration,
customers try to renew online;
it's impossible because they
are having technical problems.

"SERVICE"
After an hour of trying to find a
customer service number, a
customer orders the disk. The disk
is sent to someone else. It takes
a month to get the fix.

Popular stand-up comedian who appears on Comedy Central and HBO, Lewis Black puts it best in *Fast Company* magazine, "After all, for every customer service superstar, there remain a thousand (tens of thousands? a million?) losers. Day to day service is a string of bad blind dates, an endless series of humiliations."[3]

A big disappointment is a phone or wireless company's recording, "We're experiencing unusually high call volumes. Visit us on the Web." I thought they were in the phone business (i.e., answering phones), which means actually talking to someone.

The only service that matters is that which focuses on delivering a desired emotional feeling and experience for the customer. In other words, it doesn't really matter what you do or what you think service is; it only matters how you want your customers to feel.

PROMISES COMPARED TO MISSIONS OR VISIONS

What's the difference between a promise and a mission or vision statement? Many organizations have mission or vision statements, and some believe that it is the same as a promise. Generally, a mission or vision statement outlines what an organization is going to do. When Microsoft came into being, its early vision was "a PC on every desk and in every home." This really was an expression of their intention to lead the microcomputer business. Their vision has since changed to focus on the customer. (See Figure 2.3.)

A promise is intended to characterize how a company or organization wants its customers, members, or stakeholders to feel.

A promise is not intended to be the advertising tagline or marketing hype that seems to be the result of many branding campaigns. The promise should become the heart and soul of an organization and set the tone for everything it does. It's the internal battle cry that is intended to set an organization's expectations for every employee, agent, or representative. It dictates how the organization wants its customers to feel about their experience. The State Farm example (see Figure 2.4) indicates a commitment to being fast and efficient and a promise to be there for their customers.

IT'S ALL ABOUT HOW YOU WANT PEOPLE TO FEEL

The promise philosophy boils down to understanding that it's all about how someone feels as a customer or a guest or even as

FIGURE 2.3

Used with permission.

an employee. While it is essential to be really good at the functional side of your business, that's the given for success today. Your distinctiveness needs to be focused on how you want to make people feel.

Tim Sanders, author of *The Likeability Factor*,[4] makes it easy to understand. In his highly successful seminars, he asks

FIGURE 2.4

executives, How likeable are you? This should also apply to all
of an organization's associates, representatives, and anyone else
who works there.

At Peju wines in St. Helena, California (Napa Valley), everyone seems to understand that it's important to focus on how the
guests feel. As Tony Peju says, "Some people talk, some people do.
At Peju, we do."[5]

According to Tom McLean, director of integrated marketing
and branding for *Consumer Reports*, "A lot of companies talk
about their commitment or dedication to customers; however,
I don't know that they really understand many aspects of how
their brand is perceived." Many public companies are possessed
by a total preoccupation with their stock price. When a singular
focus on financial results occurs, it is at the expense of brand
equity in customers' minds, and this can be a precursor to failure.

Consumer Reports, published by the nonprofit organization Consumers Union, provides honest, unbiased, comparative information and services based on scientific research and consumer surveys. It provides a reality check on the all-too-prevalent hype, and it tests promises every day.

My belief is that if a brand has a real promise that's right for its customers, the company should be able to monitor the product's or service's perception, quality, and equity in a way that will make it possible for the company to foresee the outcome of a *Consumer Reports'* evaluation of the product or service before the magazine is published.

Before an organization can really commit to making a promise, it has to have the heart and a real desire to make other people happy. It seems so obvious! Why doesn't every company have the heart to make a promise? Having the heart to make a promise means that the leadership of the organization must be more emotionally focused on the customers' benefits than they are on the functional benefits. It's the concept that drove Dale Carnegie to become an icon. His philosophy in the book *How to Win Friends and Influence People*, which has sold over 10 million copies and was on the *New York Times* bestseller list for over 10 years, was based on a genuine concern for how the other person feels.

As Dale Carnegie wrote, "When dealing with people, let us remember we are not dealing with creatures of logic, we are dealing with creatures of emotion, creatures bristling with prejudices and motivated by pride and vanity."[6] While this may be harsh, it is fundamentally important.

Too many self-help books focus on what the reader wants. Dale Carnegie focused on the other person's wants and needs. He said, "Become genuinely interested in other people."[7] Developing a genuine promise and keeping it requires a basic understanding of human nature.

I think it's important to remember that impressions involve at least two or more people and that every interaction involves two components: what an organization and its representatives are doing and how the person(s) they are serving feels about the interaction. Many times the actions are forgotten, but the feeling is remembered.

Jay Leno recently commented in the foreword of *The Power of Nice: How to Conquer the Business World with Kindness,* "We live in a society where common courtesy is so uncommon that it is treated as though you just saved someone's life by giving them the Heimlich maneuver. So many of today's problems can be solved with simple acts of kindness."[8]

All too often brand discussions tend to be focused on an organization's products and services, which are just one dimension of the study of BrandScience insights.

Sunset magazine is an institution in the publishing world with a rich history of success since it was founded in 1898. Its subscription renewal rate is one of the highest in the publishing industry. What's its secret? It focuses on how it wants its readers to feel. This is not just about publishing a magazine; for *Sunset* this is about being the readers' guide to enjoying living in the West.

"It's like being the neighbor next door who knows a little more than you do, but isn't pretentious and doesn't show off accordingly," says Katie Tamony, editor in chief. She describes *Sunset*'s promise to its readers, "as being helpful, friendly, knowledgeable, like a good friend."

Sunset's team works hard at envisioning their readers in their everyday lives and then providing them with the inspiration to really enjoy every part of their life.

Sunset's commitment to enhancing its readers' lives reflects the culture of *Sunset*'s employees. It's genuine, authentic, and practical. Each year, the magazine invites its readers for a weekend at its corporate campus in Menlo Park, California. Twenty thousand people from all over the western United States come to experience the *Sunset* lifestyle up close and personal.

FIGURE 2.5

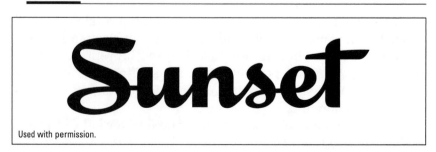

Used with permission.

ARE *YOU* READY TO MAKE A GENUINE PROMISE?

Making a genuine promise means that you and your organization are committed to how you want your customers, partners, clients, and associates to feel. We use the word genuine throughout the book to remind ourselves that a *genuine* promise is sincere, honest, heartfelt, and trustworthy.

The challenge in today's marketplace is gaining a real understanding of the word "brand" and how it relates to a promise. The concept of branding and the word itself is probably the most misunderstood and abused idea among organizations, regardless of their type or size. In my opinion, the basic misunderstanding of the true concept of brand contributed to the loss of trillions of dollars of shareholder value in the major equity markets between 1999 and 2003. Executives frequently say, "We are focused on branding," or "Yes, we are branded," or "We are going through a branding process." However, the results clearly show they are not.

Before an organization of any kind can use "brand" or "branding" as a verb, it must first develop a strategy for its brand that is based on a promise. Any so-called brand thinking must begin with the development of a BrandPromise commitment based on a covenant of trust.

A brand's promise should be at the heart of the relationship between the organization and its customers and prospective customers. Customers expect companies to do what they say they are going to do.

The key to success in any endeavor is also its sole purpose: To create delighted customers, not unsatisfactory experiences. This is true for corporations, nonprofits, religious organizations, celebrities, and even government. Putting the customer, member, client, or constituent first is not a new concept. However, it certainly is not the number one focus of many organizations today. While many organizations scramble to gain the upper hand on competitors, increase shareholder value, and struggle to retain the slimmest slice of market share, the customer is ignored—far too often.

If delighting customers is so important, then what's the motivation for organizations to ignore this fundamental concept. There are several possible reasons that organizations could

LIVING THE PROMISE

▼

It's about MAKING and KEEPING a promise with people. It goes beyond writing it down — it's about LIVING THE PROMISE!

be motivated to ignore their customers' feelings. The consolidation of many industries has provided a quasi-oligopoly or monopoly environment. As an example, while there may be three major cellular phone providers, if only one has a signal at a customer's home, the customer really has only one choice, regardless of the service.

Delighting customers involves an investment. If an organization is interested in improving financial results in the short term, customer service is often targeted.

We're not talking about customer service per se; there is a vast difference between providing customer service and *serving* the customer. And we are not talking about who has the latest fashion trend, fastest technology, or best new widget.

We are talking about *making* and *keeping* a promise with people whether they are customers, prospective customers, clients, members, constituents, or stakeholders. Writing a promise is one thing; living it is quite another. It's about treating people right and treating them better than they expect to be treated.

THE PROMISERULE

THE PROMISERULE

▼

Treat others BETTER than they EXPECT to be TREATED!

Everyone's heard of the Golden Rule: Do unto others as you would have others do unto you. While the Golden Rule is important, we believe that it's time to raise the bar. The new standard for genuine brands is the PromiseRule: Treat others *better* than they expect to be treated. Success and competitive advantage are all about exceeding customers' expectations.

The PromiseRule represents the single greatest opportunity for small businesses as well as corporations, nonprofits, entrepreneurs, and professional service providers to do more than survive. It affords them the strategic weapon to distinguish themselves in the marketplace, providing them the opportunity to prosper long term, and it provides customers with pleasant surprises.

Customers interact with organizations on many levels and in a variety of ways, the most common of which is through the actual use of a product or service. It is this usage experience that ultimately determines and forges customer perceptions. Remember that we're dealing with not only packaged products; we're dealing with services too. In today's economic environment, services are the primary products of many organizations. No longer can organizations think in terms of producing world-class products without thinking about delivering world-class experiences. Products and service are inextricably linked. Figure 2.6 provides a quick test for any organization to evaluate their customer experiences.

FIGURE 2.6

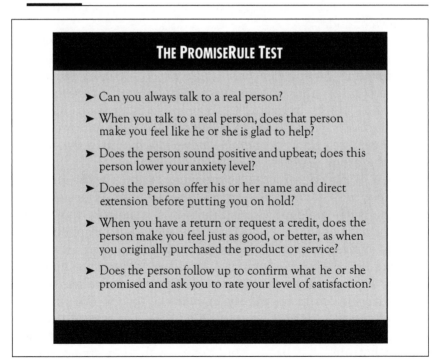

THE PROMISERULE TEST

➤ Can you always talk to a real person?

➤ When you talk to a real person, does that person make you feel like he or she is glad to help?

➤ Does the person sound positive and upbeat; does this person lower your anxiety level?

➤ Does the person offer his or her name and direct extension before putting you on hold?

➤ When you have a return or request a credit, does the person make you feel just as good, or better, as when you originally purchased the product or service?

➤ Does the person follow up to confirm what he or she promised and ask you to rate your level of satisfaction?

Perceptions, once formed, are difficult to alter, much less manipulate. The heavy burden for all enterprises, regardless of size or market, is this: It is the customer who decides whether a brand's product or service has value. The brand's promise and the organization's ability to deliver on that promise ultimately determine its success.

This is why many of the dot-coms failed. They did not have a promise. Or if they made one, chances are it was broken. During the height of the initial e-commerce surge on the Internet, how many e-commerce sites offered free shipping with the promise of delivery in time for Christmas? How many could not deliver on that promise? The vast majority of them never saw the next holiday shopping season. Why? Because they found out too late that once a promise was made, people expected them not only to keep it but make good on it as well if the promise was broken.

Internet companies were not alone in the unfulfilled promise department. Many companies fail to provide personal service when it is needed most. How easy is it to contact a real "live" empowered, decision-making customer service representative on the weekends?

It is the experience—the interaction between customers and the company—that shapes and drives brand perceptions, attitudes, and buying decisions. This process begins when the promise is made and extends to when the promise is delivered. The brand's ability to live up to its promise determines whether customers, newly acquired or long term, are loyal and return. It also determines how frequently they return. But most importantly the promise determines how they feel.

New York Life's media advertising expresses the promise philosophy well. Its advertising asks the question, "Does a promise come with an expiration date? Is it a month, a year, or decades from now? At New York Life we make promises that have no expiration date." (See Figure 2.7.)

The successful implementation of an innovative and distinctive strategy for any organization's brand, regardless of size, are tightly linked to its ability to succeed beyond the first few years of operation—and prosper as well. At the end of the day, brands that live their promise have the opportunity to enjoy a healthy bottom line. Brands that don't—well, they spend a lot of

FIGURE 2.7

Does a promise come with
an expiration date? Is it a month,
a year, or decades from now?
At NEW YORK LIFE we make
promises that have no
expiration date.

Reprinted with permission.

time and energy wondering why their bottom line is eroding. To these and organizations like them, being branded means that they have a logo; it doesn't mean that they have a strategy and it usually means that they don't have a promise. The true essence of a genuine brand is its promise.

A GUARANTEE THAT'S REAL

I have always believed that the first measure of a promise is whether or not a company or organization actually stands behind it. It's easy to say, "We have a promise," especially if everything's going smoothly. But what happens when things are not going right?

This is where the guarantee comes in. In the retail world, this is generally called the "return policy." This is the actual company policy that tells associates how they are supposed to handle returns. If you've ever read one, the language can be very complex and resembles that of an insurance policy.

Our concept of a guarantee is based on a philosophy of signals. Promise signals can include everything from the cleanliness of the restrooms to the attitude of the cashiers at a store or the customer service representatives on the phone. The most important promise signal can be an organization's commitment to how they make the customers feel when they have a product or service problem or need help.

Ace Hardware is a good example of the value of a no-hassle guarantee. When I return an item to Ace, I'm never made to feel bad, nor do I get a hassle. In fact, Ace makes customers feel just as good about the return as they did about the original purchase. This is a *service* signal.

Ace is actually a cooperative of 4,600 stores owned primarily by individual operators, and the company has recently enjoyed great success. As Ray Griffith, the CEO, says, "We come to work every day on behalf of the entrepreneur. We have a chip on our shoulder about the big boxes, and we like that. We like being the underdog. America loves the underdog."[9] It's clear that Ace wants to distinguish its customer experience from other "big box" stores (national home improvement megastores).

It's interesting to note that in 2007 Ace Hardware (The Helpful Place) was ranked the highest in customer satisfaction for major home improvement stores by J.D. Power and Associates.[10]

Another great example is Wolferman's. Wolferman's was founded in 1888 and has been a proud purveyor of specialty foods for over 100 years. In 1910 it started making the unique English muffins, which is only one of their premium specialty foods. Wolferman's promise to its customers is to, "Deliver exceptional food experiences to our valued customers."[11] You'll notice in Figure 2.8 that Wolferman's expresses its commitment to making its customers feel "delighted."

I believe that if you exceed the customer's expectations, you can succeed against the corporate goliaths. And, once again, a no-hassle guarantee is a moneymaker.

It's always great when someone responds to a request with; "It's my pleasure." At the world famous La Quinta Resort in La

FIGURE 2.8

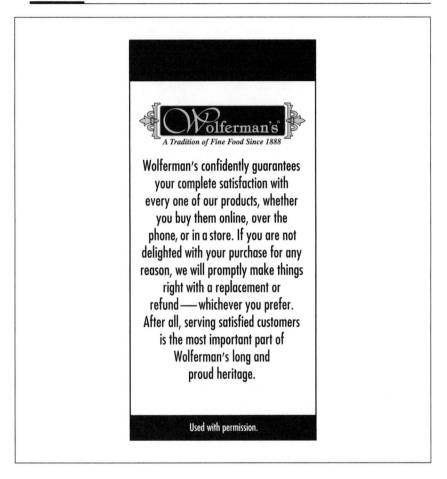

Quinta, California, phone calls are always answered with, "It's a beautiful day at the La Quinta Resort."

The concept of "it's my pleasure" reminds me of the famous promise signal "make it so" that Captain Jean-Luc Picard used on the television series *Star Trek: The Next Generation.* "Make it so" is a great reminder of how to make customers feel.

A guarantee is not necessarily about an advertisement or a public proclamation, but it is all about signaling to the customer that an organization's commitment to exceed its expectations is real.

If we could hear everything customers say about a business or organization, what kind of feelings would they have? Customers would most likely consider their entire history of experiences with an organization whether it was a few months or several years. How would your customers answer these questions?

- Do they feel genuinely welcome upon arrival?
- Was their most recent experience better than their previous experiences?
- Did they experience a pleasant surprise; something that made them feel special?
- Did they feel good about the way an issue was resolved?

Customers want to feel special, not just good. They want to tell their family and friends about some part of their experience that was really enjoyable, fun, unique, or exceptional. Most importantly, the most recent customer experience determines the "share of the customer's wallet" that a business will receive in the future.

Making customers feel good is much more than the right thing to do. Customer satisfaction can be a very smart financial strategy. The American Customer Satisfaction Index (ACSI) is a collaboration of the University of Michigan Business School and the American Society for Quality. They conduct 70,000 consumer interviews annually. According to the director of the ACSI, "No doubt about it, satisfied customers make a difference to companies ... We have very, very strong empirical findings that companies with satisfied customers do much better in terms of economic performance, whether it's profits, stock prices or some other measure of shareholder value."[12]

Organizations face challenges every day, and problems are always possible. The issue is not whether or not there may be a problem in the customer's mind; the issue is how a brand makes customers feel during the interaction to find a solution. This is a fundamental point that's missed by many customer service representatives. When representatives start explaining the policy, they are beginning to lose the customer.

The following Brand Profile on Costco illustrates the advantage to an organization that makes and keeps its promises.

BRAND PROFILE

COSTCO

GENUINE BRANDS MAKE A PROMISE

Genuine brands, like Costco, change the paradigm in their business sector. In other words, they change the model in their business so that they become perceived as a distinctive and one-of-a-kind retailer—not just one of many.

In late 2006, Costco opened its 500th warehouse in La Quinta, California, near Palm Springs. To those who have been with the company since it opened its first warehouse on September 15, 1983, in a commercial district of Seattle, this milestone is astonishing. Back then, membership warehouse clubs were a new concept, as was the idea of a no-frills, bare-bones retail environment.

From the beginning, Costco founders Jim Sinegal and Jeffrey Brotman believed that if they offered successful brand-name products at the lowest prices and if they treated suppliers and employees well, with lots of hard work their business could succeed. But they had no idea that Costco would eventually have nearly 50 million members, with operations across the United States, Canada, and Mexico as well as overseas in the United Kingdom, Korea, Taiwan, and Japan.

Costco owes part of its heritage to the Price Club, a membership warehouse chain that opened its first store in San Diego in 1976. In 1993, Costco and the Price Club merged, operating as Price/Costco until 1997, when the company changed its name to Costco.

FIGURE 2.9

Used with permission.

"The business has become significantly more complicated over the years," says Costco president and CEO Jim Sinegal. "We had no pharmacies, optical centers, gas stations, fresh meat, or produce. We took cash or checks only. We didn't even have hot dogs the first year."[13]

But Sinegal says that, despite Costco's many changes, most of the company's original core operating concepts remain intact.

Let's examine Costco's promise and see how it has propelled its success. I believe that while Costco could be considered a discount retailer, like Target or even Wal-Mart, Costco owns a position of its own. Costco has really earned the unique position of "my purchasing agent." Whether it's items for resale among its small business members or members buying for their home, the perception is the same; I trust Costco to buy the right things for me.

As anyone knows who worked for large companies in the past, it was commonplace to go to the purchasing agent to get supplies, raw materials, and anything else that was needed. The agent would negotiate the best price for the quality items that were needed. The purchasing agent looked out for the company's and employees' interests.

Costco has earned this same kind of trust by promising an experience built around exceptional value. Exceptional perceived value is not just about lowest price; it's the optimum combination of how the customer (member) feels, the time involved, and the price paid. Costco is a genius at achieving this perception of exceptional value in its members' minds. The perception begins with the emotional side of Costco's intent—to make you feel good!

A WORLD-CLASS GUARANTEE

It's simple at Costco. You bring back something you're not happy with; no problem. The company cheerfully gives you your money back *in cash!** No store credits, coupons, "buy backs," or other hassles. Most importantly, it's how Costco wants to make you feel—as good as the original purchase. That's the key. How many

---

*Costco allows returns on electronic equipment within 90 days and offers a
  two-year extended warranty.

FIGURE 2.10

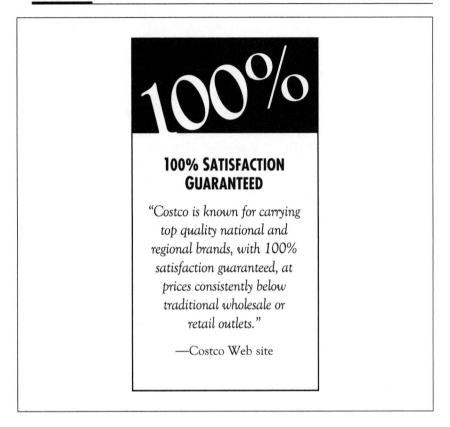

retailers cheerfully refund your purchase price in cash, even if you paid with a credit card? Costco's mindset is evidenced by its chief financial officer, Richard Galanti's statement, "If we are going to make a change (in their return policy), we want it to be the best policy out there."

CREATING A VALUED PRIVATE BRAND, NOT PRIVATE LABELS

Costco's philosophy on its own brand, Kirkland, is very different from other retailers' historical private-label approach. The industry's approach has been to create private labels that will sell with higher margins than the national brands and therefore make more money.

Costco's Kirkland brand is about quality as you would expect; however, Costco raised the bar in the industry. If you buy Kirkland's Tuscan olive oil, Brut champagne, or Chardonnay wine, you can count on it tasting at the top end of the flavor scale. Many retailers focus on the lowest price and highest margin without concern for taste. Kirkland's food products deliver the flavor of a private high-quality brand, not just a low price. Think about this: 40 percent of the Tuscan olive oil sold in the United States in 2005 was the Kirkland brand.[14]

Recently, the Costco magazine for members, *The Costco Connection*, included an article titled, "Champagne Chronicles." In two pages, you could learn everything you would want to know about champagne.

Interestingly enough, it's clear that Costco knows the ins and outs of real French champagne, and the article isn't just a one-sided view of why the Kirkland brand is a great choice. It really analyzes the paradigm shifts created by Dom Pérignon and Veuve Clicquot. Consider this: Costco is the leading seller of Dom Pérignon in the United States.

Here's the real kicker: large retailers and brands spend millions of dollars in media advertising to promote their brands, yet Costco doesn't advertise. Why? Because it doesn't have to. When your promise is right, your customers, or in Costco's case, its members, know it.

WHAT ABOUT TIME?

Editing saves time. Costco figured it out. Grocery stores, on average, carry between 40,000 and 60,000 SKUs (stock keeping units). Costco averages about 4,000. Yet the perception is that it's a warehouse and that there are lots of choices. That perception is what counts. Who needs seven different brands of nuts? Costco's deluxe mixed nuts are the best; who needs another choice. If a member needs an item, Costco will figure it out, and this superb editing does save time.

TRUST WITH A CAPITAL T

A major TV news network visited several major food retailers to review their food safety practices. According to the investigation, the network found several problems with most of the large retailers. However, when confronted by the media's conclusions, many major U.S. food retailers sent their form letters outlining their commitment to food safety. None of them would provide an executive to discuss the network's findings; except one—Costco. Jim Sinegal, the president and CEO of Costco, appeared in a Costco store thanking the media for their insights and checking temperatures of food coolers to make sure they were appropriate.

It's these kinds of down-to-earth genuine values that earn Costco the trust prize. It is also not surprising that Costco sets a ceiling on its pricing over wholesale costs to continue to earn its members' trust, unlike most retailers who will price products at whatever they think the market will bear without regard for the consumers' long-term perception.

FIGURE 2.11

FOOD SAFETY

Jim explains, "All of us in the
retail food business are very
concerned about food safety.
We want our members
to know that we would address
any concerns."

—Jim Sinegal,
President & CEO

Costco has earned its own branded descriptor for its members' shopping experience; the "Costco Run." And yet almost everyone seems to say that they spent more than they planned; how does this happen? The members' perception is clearly that they feel really good about Costco's value proposition, and that's the key to trusting Costco. This is why its members renew their memberships at the rate of nearly 87 percent. Costco's commitment to its employees and members brings its promise to life.

THOUGHT GUIDE

THE PROMISERULE—ENHANCING PEOPLE'S LIVES

- The key questions are:
  - Does every person associated with a brand know what the promise is?
  - Does every associate know how he or she is supposed to deliver the promise?
- Service means nothing unless it's connected to how a brand wants its customers to feel.
- A promise focuses on how an organization or individual wants its customers to feel, while missions or visions usually relate to what an organization expects to do.
- A genuine brand that has a real promise should know how its customers feel every day and not have to wait for a rating service to determine its customer satisfaction.
- So-called branding initiatives that do not include a real promise are a waste of time and money.
- The PromiseRule: "Treat customers better than they expect to be treated.
- The PromiseRule test:
  - Can customers always talk to a real person?
  - When customers talk to associates, do the associates make the customers feel that they are glad to help?
  - Do associates sound positive and upbeat in order to lower customer anxiety levels?

- ○ Do associates offer their name and direct extension before they place customers on hold?
- ○ When customers have to return a product or request a credit, do associates make them feel just as good, or better, than when the customer originally purchased the product or service?
- ○ Do associates follow up to confirm that what they promised was delivered and ask customers to rate their level of satisfaction?
- A brand's guarantee should go hand in hand with making customers feel great. A guarantee is much more than just standing behind a product.

CHAPTER 3

The Roadmap to a BrandPromise Commitment

A promise made is a debt unpaid.
—Robert W. Service

A PROMISE FOCUS

A paradigm shift in thinking can create a change in an organization's focus from products or services to promise-based experiences. The BrandPromise methodology is a significant contributor to this new approach. A *Harvard Business Review* article describes this as, "A sea change in managerial attitudes from a product-centric to a promise-centric business model."[1]

THE BRAND BALANCE

As we outlined in the first two chapters, it's essential to have the right mindset before an organization can make a genuine promise. (See Figure 3.1.) This perspective is enhanced by an understanding of the Brand Balance shown in Figure 3.2.

A person's perception of any brand, business, or personal experience can be divided into two aspects: functional and emotional.

FIGURE 3.1

FIGURE 3.2

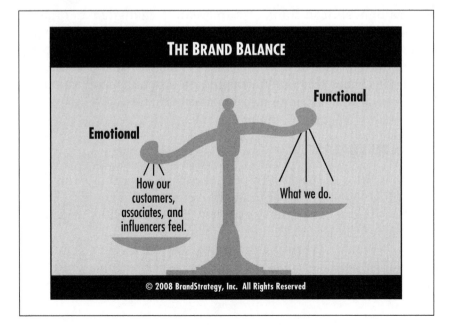

Most often when we audit executives' activities, we find that most of their focus is usually on the "functional" side of their business. These activities include product or service quality, financial issues, day-to-day operational priorities, and the like. These functional priorities are, of course, extremely important, and an organization must be really proficient at its functional business if it is to be successful.

Genuine brands know that they must excel at their functional business; this must be a given. However, the focus of their promise and their ultimate success as a genuine brand must be on their "emotional" benefits to their *stakeholders* (associates, customers, consumers, and influencers.) Long-term differentiation is achieved on the emotional side of the brand perception equation.

In developing a promise for your organization, there is an important theorem that must be applied before the process begins. This theorem is known as the Feel→Do Law. Traditionally, organizations have focused on what associates are supposed to *do*—in other words, their jobs or functional responsibilities. Associates' feelings or the customers' feelings are often absent or of secondary importance.

FIGURE 3.3

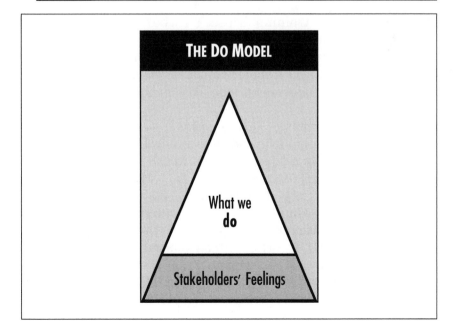

FIGURE 3.4

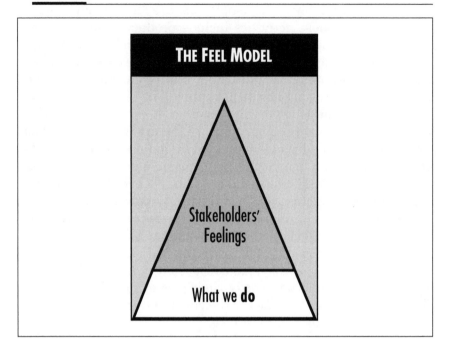

As an example, most so-called customer service programs or customer service training focuses on what the associates are supposed to do, that is, how they are supposed to do their respective jobs, as illustrated in Figure 3.3. Much more attention should be focused on how the organization wants its associates, customers, and influencers to feel. This is the "Feel" model as outlined in Figure 3.4.

Feelings are most important because they are the key to brand success! Canadian Broadcasting news reported recently that a brand's equity is "deeply rooted in the brain."

Christine Born, a radiologist at Munich's Ludwig-Maximilians University Hospital, said, "We found that strong brands activate certain areas of the brain independent of product categories."[2] Researchers found that the familiar brands activated a network of cortical areas related to emotional processing and linked with self-identification and rewards.

In late 2002, Longs Drug Stores recruited Warren Bryant, a successful senior executive officer at Kroger, to become president and chief executive officer. He immediately began to focus on customers' perceptions of their retail experience at Longs.

As Warren explains, "A company's promise must create a feeling of trust, and trust comes from how you make your customers feel." A key part of Longs' strategy was to establish service-related metrics which would be used to build the right customer experience. Longs' analysis concluded that stores with customer service ratings of 70 percent or higher earned a positive same-store sales increase of 1.7 percent. Stores with service ratings of less than 70 percent experienced a decline in same-store sales. Figure 3.5 outlines the correlation between the customer's experience and same-store sales, which is linked to profitability.

"This customer experience information was one of the key factors that provided a foundation for Longs to enhance their brand experience. In addition, Longs also focuses on the customer's experience when there is a problem. It's extremely important that your associates have the mindset that every problem is

FIGURE 3.5

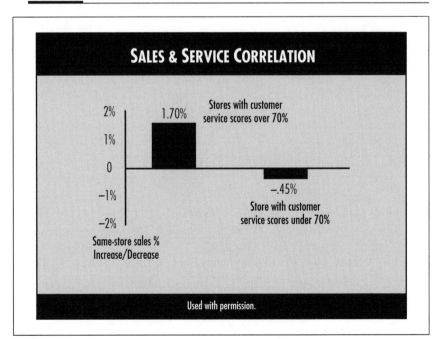

SALES & SERVICE CORRELATION

Used with permission.

an opportunity to reinforce your relationship with the customer," says Bryant. Longs calls this its recovery strategy. No one can run a business without having problems. If an organization employs the right recovery strategy, it can really differentiate a brand and create long-term trust in the customer's mind.

"Longs' focus on their customer's experience was a contributor to a financial turnaround resulting in a 126% increase in their stock price between 2002 and 2007," according to the company.

CHANGING THE DECISION HIERARCHY

All too often, the brand decision hierarchy follows the operational hierarchy as shown in Figure 3.6. Basically, a small number of executives may actually decide customer policies or procedures. During a merger or acquisition, the customer's best interests can be ignored. As an example, a large retail chain

FIGURE 3.6

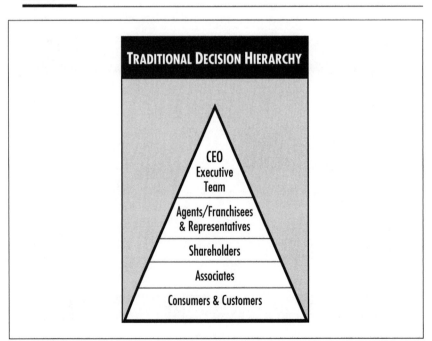

acquired a regional retail brand, and the chain promoted the benefit of being able to launch a national advertising campaign and a new distribution strategy while changing the name of the acquired brand. Instead of providing better customer service or other initiatives that would improve its customers' lives, the new policies instituted at the acquired stores after the acquisition actually alienated associates and customers and resulted in decreased sales.

In fact, most mergers and acquisitions are about money or size and are rarely about improving the experience or promise for the customers. More surprisingly, most mergers or acquisitions have not produced the expected or promised shareholder returns.

A recent review of 180 studies of mergers and acquisitions over the last 20 years, conducted by Robert F. Bruner at the University of Virginia, determined that 65.6 percent—nearly two-thirds—of all transactions failed. Failure not only included substandard results but, in almost half of the merger and acquisitions considered failures—or one-third of all transactions— value was actually destroyed.[3]

The reason for this can be discovered in consumers' perceptions. Most mergers are announced with the fanfare of a Fourth of July parade, which always includes the formulaic language, "It will be seamless to our customers," or "There will be no effect on our customers' experience." Unfortunately, consumers' perceptions, developed after many bad experiences, tell the real story. We've asked thousands of consumers whether their experience as a customer of a merged, purged, consolidated, or acquired brand such as a phone company, utility, retailer, bank, or airline improved after the transaction. Answer: not one indicated that service improved.

If a brand merger or acquisition is to succeed, it first must be perceived as a positive benefit or positive in the minds of customers and consumers. The decision hierarchy must be turned upside down as illustrated in Figure 3.7.

Customers and consumers should be at the forefront of every corporate or organizational decision. If customers' perception of a brand's experience is not improved or at least consistent with their service experience before a merger or acquisition, then the brand may be at risk.

FIGURE 3.7

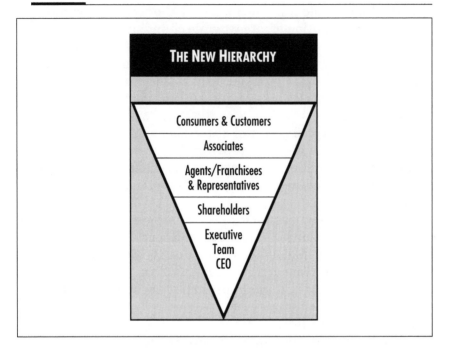

Think of a major merger or acquisition in the automotive, retail, telecommunications, or media business over the last five years. Which of those mergers produced a better or "one of a kind" experience for customers or improved the quality or distinctiveness?

Many corporate transactions are about getting bigger and, unfortunately, not about getting better. The explanation is simply based on economics. Company A wants to get bigger, so it acquires Company B. Company A wants Company B because it has a good brand in consumers' minds driven by its customer service reputation. In order to acquire Company B, Company A must pay a premium over its current value. After Company A pays the premium and acquires Company B, it must pay for the acquisition cost. Company A then cuts Company B's costs including employees in order to increase the profit margin and net income. Company B's net income increases over the short term while customer service declines. Then customers become dissatisfied with the changes, and sales begin to drop as a result of a declining brand.

Northwestern Mutual Insurance Company clearly understands the need to focus on better, not biggest. "The ambition of Northwestern has been less to be large than safe; its aim is to rank first in benefits to policy owners rather than first in size."[4]

Northwestern's promise has paid off. It enjoys one of the highest "persistency ratios" in the life insurance business. Edward Zore, the president and chief executive officer, says, "We view persistency as a measure of customer satisfaction calculated by the percentage of customers who keep their policies in place each year. Our persistency ratio has risen to 96.5%, one of the best in the industry."[5]

THE PROMISE PROCESS

The promise process includes four steps:

1. Create a BrandPromise team.
2. Complete the Brand Assessment.
3. Develop a brand's promise.
4. Communicate and culturalize the promise.

An initiative to develop a new or energized promise must be inspired by one of the senior executive officers of an organization. Unless the president, chief executive officer, chairperson, executive director, or the equivalent establishes the importance of a promise, it most likely will not become a reality. Many of our clients have included a board member as part of the process, which has universally led to great success. A brand team should be developed with fewer than 10 executives, managers, and associates representing a cross section of the organization's operations. The members of the brand team should be the "best and brightest" of an organization's representatives. They should be varied by position, level, and area of responsibility, and they should include operations, front-line, marketing, finance, and so on. It typically can take four to six months to develop a promise depending on the size and complexity of an organization. The promise team should commission the appropriate research so that it can objectively assess how a brand is currently perceived as well as how it would want to be perceived.

We recommend that a research plan be developed that includes a representative sample of all of a brand's various stakeholders.

The Brand Assessment research outlined below should identify attribute perceptions from three perspectives.

1. Absolute perceptions
2. Relative perceptions compared to other choices
3. Best demonstrated practices

Absolute perceptions are all about how consumers, customers, associates, and influencers feel about a specific brand. The term "relative perceptions" refers to their comparisons of a brand to other choices. The term "best demonstrated practices" examines other organizations that excel in delivering a desired attribute such as product, service, value, or other experiential attribute. In most cases, the best demonstrated practices will be discovered in other industries or applications.

This research and other evaluations provide the information necessary to complete the assessment phase of developing a promise. A detailed outline of the Brand Assessment process is provided in Chapter 10.

The promise should reflect a balance between the aspirations of the brand and the reality of what the brand is capable of delivering to its customers. It's important to remember that a promise should be aspirational enough to inspire a brand's associates. Also, successful promises migrate over time to fulfill customers' changing desires. Figure 3.8 outlines the promise purpose and process.

Developing a promise is just the beginning. Once a promise has been finalized, a comprehensive communication "buy-in" and training program will also need to be developed and implemented for all existing associates. Regularly scheduled culturalization training sessions will need to be organized for all new associates. The initial training may take several months, depending on an organization's size or complexity, and is outlined in more detail in Chapter 10. The internal responsibility for implementing a promise is a long-term responsibility, not this year's campaign or the new idea of the month.

FIGURE 3.8

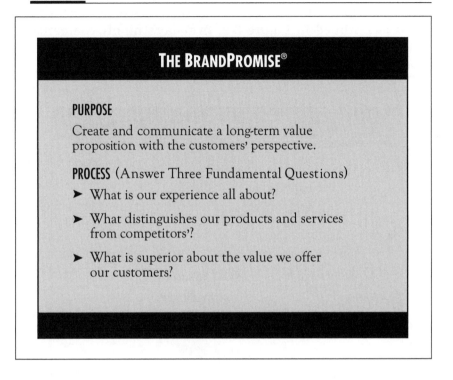

The Brand Profiles provided throughout this book can help guide the implementation of a brand's promise.

ASSESSING CUSTOMERS' FEELINGS

One of the foundations for developing a strong and distinctive brand promise is to understand how consumers and customers feel. It is especially helpful to understand not only what motivates choice and behavior but also where a brand resides in the Brand Spectrum.

Understanding what motivates consumers to choose one brand over another helps identify which functional and emotional benefits are the "cost of entry" and which can make a brand distinctive in the market. Kathy Fredell, president of Fredell Consulting, developed a system which can clearly identify which attributes are the *cost of entry*—in other words, attributes consumers require in a brand to consider it versus attributes that can make a brand distinctive in consumers' minds as outlined in Figure 3.9. In today's highly competitive

FIGURE 3.9

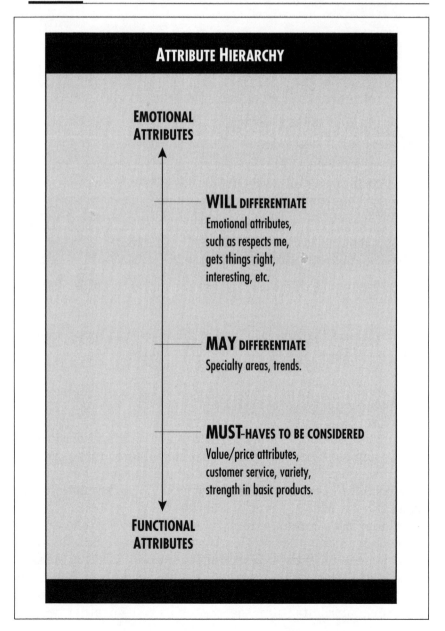

markets, the attributes which differentiate a brand are emotional rather than functional (i.e., makes my family happy, rather than low price). For example, in a recent study of a retail chain, the following hierarchy of decision making was identified. The attributes actually identified have been collapsed into categories.

Many of the functional attributes are the cost of entry. In contrast, the true differentiators are emotionally based. As a result, the success of genuine brands depends on the emotional link they can make with consumers. Identification of the attribute hierarchy is very helpful in the development of a promise by identifying which attributes are needed for differentiation.

A second key step in developing a distinct and differentiated promise is to understand what type of relationship consumers have with your brand and with key competitors. Is it more functionally driven, resulting in little to no differentiation and customer loyalty? Or is it more emotionally driven, resulting in strong differentiation and loyalty? The stronger the emotional ties with your brand, the stronger the customer loyalty. Conversely, if few emotional links exist with your brand, consumers are more functionally driven and can more easily be persuaded to choose another brand. Fredell Consulting developed a brand spectrum which identifies the emotional links consumers have with a brand and with its competitors. The brand spectrum combines a variety of information about a brand and its competitors as illustrated in Figure 3.10. This is an example of the brand spectrum for a retail chain. Each circled letter represents a different competitor.

Notice that four of the competitors (F, G, H, and I) operate at the functional level. This means that they have to constantly reinforce their relationship with consumers, usually through pricing adjustments and promotions. The four competitors with functional positions reflect a lack of a distinct and strong promise. Without a strong emotional link with consumers, these competitors have to focus on maintaining store traffic (or package purchases) and must constantly reinforce their relationship with shoppers.

In contrast, competitors A and B have strong emotional relationships with consumers. They are often described by shoppers as exciting, respectful, and trusting at levels unparalleled

FIGURE 3.10

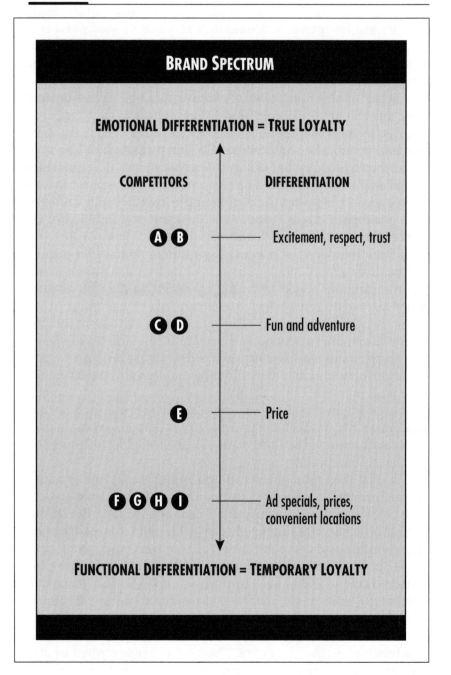

in most retail environments. This reflects their successful implementation of a strong promise. The benefit is that competitors with strong emotional links already have strong loyalty among shoppers and do not need to use excessive marketing dollars to generate store traffic. Competitors A and B, with strong emotional ties, experienced increased sales and expanded their outlets, while those at the functional end of the brand spectrum struggled to increase sales.

As you can see, understanding consumer motivations, the attributes which can differentiate a brand and a brand's perceptions compared to its competitors' positions on the brand spectrum, can be very helpful in developing a strong promise. While there are many indicators that can determine a brand's perceptions, we like to include the following four areas in research studies:

- Distinctiveness
- Relevance
- Perceived value
- Overall experience

Distinctiveness refers to how distinctive a brand's products and services are perceived in everyone's minds—consumers, customers, associates, and influencers. The second indicator reflects how stakeholders perceive the *relevance* of a brand's offerings related to their needs and desires. *Perceived value* relates to the combination of consumers' perceptions of benefits compared to the cost which includes time, feelings, and money. *Overall experience* measures perceptions of a brand's customer transactions and identifies gaps between the opinions of associates and customers.

MAKING A PROMISE

A promise places the customer first. It is a state of mind, the heart and soul of an organization. A promise defines how an organization wants its customers to feel. It defines the benefits, both emotional and functional, that the customers should expect to receive when experiencing a brand's products or services.

BRANDPROMISE® DEFINITION

▼

The essence (heart, soul, and spirit) of the functional and emotional benefits that customers and influencers receive when experiencing a brand's products and services.

In order for a promise to be effective, it must be delivered at the "customer's convenience." In other words, if an organization promises to be fast or the most responsive, it must be perceived by the customers as fast.

A promise is not usually the advertising message; however, it should drive every activity and communication throughout an organization. It doesn't matter if an organization is a family business, global corporation, nonprofit, association, or entrepreneurship. The process is the same.

If an entity has a good mission statement that explains what it does, then the mission statement can coexist with a promise that defines how an organization wants its customers to feel. Scott Smith of Haggen Food & Pharmacy describes this mindset from a customer's point of view: "I don't care how much you know until I know how much you care."

Based on the perceptual insights developed in a brand's research with consumers, customers, associates, and influencers, the goal is to address the following three questions, which were introduced in Figure 3.8 earlier in this chapter.

- What is our experience all about?
- What distinguishes our products and services from competitors'?
- What is superior about the value we offer our customers?

However, in order to develop the right promise, an organization must adopt a customer-focused mindset. According to an article in *Marketing News,* "The shift to customer centricity requires that organizations not only listen to and capture customers' interactions but actually take action on what they learn."[6]

It is all about objectivity. A research process should be designed to characterize a brand's current perceptions based on factual information and data as well as observable conclusions in a manner that rules out subjective influences (such as gut feelings, intuition, opinions, etc.). Think of it as an audit, required to verify the condition of the organization's brand image, position, and perception. Then determine "where it is" in the minds of associates, customers, consumers, and influencers. It's impossible for an organization to execute a future strategy if it doesn't know objectively how its brand is perceived today. A brand can't move toward achieving its goal to be a genuine brand without a thorough understanding of customers (obtained through research), the business environment, its marketing strategy (what's worked, what hasn't, and why or why not), consumer behavior (transaction analysis), market and competitive trends, and so on.

DEFINING A BRAND'S EXPERIENCE

Defining the desired customer's experience and resulting feelings begins with separating the typical organization's process mentality. Here's an example:

In the health-care business, doctors, clinics, hospitals, pharmacies, and the like should understand that every patient has the same desire to feel better or feel his or her best. Unfortunately, many health-care businesses can become focused on the process: check in, fill out forms, insurance information, wait, wait, and more waiting. How much of the transaction with a health-care provider of any type is focused on making sure that patients feel their best? Many veterinarians and car dealers call their customers after every visit to make sure customers were satisfied. What about health care providers?

If you are in the health-care business and want to be a genuine brand, then your entire focus must be on making sure your patients feel better or the best they can feel. The Mayo Clinic was founded in 1914 by the Mayo brothers promise, "The needs of the patient come first." Figure 3.11 outlines the Mayo Clinic's commitment.

When you see this kind of promise, the true test is in the experience. How is it that their clinics see hundreds of patients a day and maintain an exceptional "on-time" performance, but

FIGURE 3.11

🛡️ **MAYO CLINIC**

THE NEEDS OF THE PATIENT COME FIRST

A team approach that relies on a
variety of medical specialists working together
to provide the highest-quality care.

An unhurried examination of each and
every patient with time to listen to the patient.

Physicians taking personal responsibility
for directing patient care in partnership with
the patient's local physician.

The highest-quality care delivered with
compassion and trust.

Respect for the patient, family and the
patient's local physician.

Comprehensive evaluation with timely,
efficient assessment and treatment.

Availability of the most advanced, innovative
diagnostic and therapeutic technologies
and techniques.

Used with permission.

when you go to a local doctor, you wait an hour? The answer: It's all about a different promise—the Mayo Clinic "respects the patient's time."

This doesn't mean that an organization shouldn't execute its process. In fact it's required. You need to be the best at your process so you can focus on the unique emotional experience for your customers that will set you apart from others. Figure 3.12 illustrates the shift from process to experience.

The goal is to identify in two or three words the experience you can deliver that will create a distinctive, one-of-a-kind perception in your customers' minds.

Husqvarna was founded in 1689 to build muskets for the king of Sweden's army. Harnessing its expertise in engines, the company began building chain saws in 1959 and offers a wide variety of outdoor vehicles and equipment for lawns, trees, and construction applications. Loggers, arborists, landscapers, farmers, and, of course, homeowners use Husqvarna's power equipment for their forest, lawn, and garden needs.

FIGURE 3.12

THE SHIFT FROM PROCESS TO EXPERIENCE

BRAND	PROCESS	EXPERIENCE
AAA	Auto service/insurance	Peace of mind
LENSCRAFTERS	Selling glasses/contacts	See better in about one hour
OPRAH	Talk show host	Trusted friend
IN-N-OUT	Hamburgers	Fresh & friendly
WHOLE FOODS	Retail grocery	Enjoy a healthy life

While Husqvarna's products are highly regarded, its promise is much more bold. "Our commitment—from every Husqvarna associate and our more than 23,000 retailers worldwide—is to provide you with a 'Great Experience.'"[7]

Many equipment manufacturers claim to produce quality products. However, what consumers and professionals appreciate is knowing that they will indeed enjoy a "great experience."

Another example of focusing on the experience is Riedel Crystal. For 250 years, the Riedel family has been making fine crystal, and the business has survived wars and turmoil to produce more than 130 crystal designs to hold every type of beverage from wine to scotch.

Its quality and reputation is legendary. However, what's really interesting is how it thinks about the business. Georg Riedel, who runs the business today, exhibits the understanding that a product is really only as good as the experience. In other words, Riedel believes that what's most important about a new Riedel crystal design is the unusual experience it will provide when someone enjoys a specific type of beverage.

Recently, the *Robb Report* magazine provided an in-depth look at how Riedel creates a new piece of glassware. Georg Riedel assembles a professional panel of experts to guide the development of a new Riedel glass, and then the adventure begins. The panel follows a very disciplined approach to develop a new product.

Riedel's philosophy on flavor relates to the four tasting zones of the tongue: Humans taste sweetness at the tip of their tongues, bitterness at the back, and sourness and saltiness on the sides. "Glasses with a lip deliver to the tip of the tongue; those with a narrow mouth send the liquid to the back," says Riedel. "A lip also delivers a narrow stream of liquid, whereas fuller, closed glasses offer a rounded sip that makes more contact with the sides of the tongue. The objective, he says, is to position the liquid so that it hits the part of the tongue that will deemphasize the beverage's overt characteristics and harmonize the 'interplay of fruit and acid.'"[8]

According to the 2006 Harley-Davidson annual report, James Ziemer, president and chief executive officer, describes the company's commitment: "As we look to the future, everyone in the Harley-Davidson family of employees remains passionate and dedicated to delivering great value and great experiences for our customers and investors."[9]

Successful brands understand that delivering an experience is much more important than just selling products and services. They must constantly reinvent themselves to ensure their relevance in their stakeholders' minds. A new product or service is not enough; organizations need to enhance customers' perceived emotional benefits as well.

DISTINCTIVE PRODUCTS AND SERVICES

The second step in the development of a promise is to identify, develop, maintain, or enhance a brand's products' or services' distinctive characteristics. Distinction is a positive connotation, including special qualities, style, or attractiveness resulting in a perceptual difference in the nature or prominence of something:

- Separateness—not being the same
- Difference in nature or quality
- Prominence, clarity to the senses
- Superiority, notable
- Conspicuousness, eminence, excellence

A promise should be aspirational and invoke a positive feeling as well as a sense of pride. The promise process should be focused on identifying, communicating, and delivering a brand's distinctive characteristics, those that are important to all its stakeholders and especially to its customers and prospective customers.

Distinctive characteristics must be beneficial to the customer. The problem today is that many organizations' intended differentiation holds little meaning for customers. If a brand desires to be distinctive, there are endless possibilities and countless options. The secret is to select or develop distinctive attributes that customers and prospective customers will value most and prefer over other choices. As an example, if an organization is in the food business (human or pet), food safety is a real opportunity to be distinctive. Daily food safety checks of products certified by an independent laboratory could provide a real

FIGURE 3.13

IN-N-OUT BURGER

"Give customers the freshest, highest quality foods you can buy and provide them with friendly service in a sparkling clean environment."

Used with permission.

perceived distinction. From spinach to dog food, it could make the difference between preferred or panned.

The concept of "organic" food has changed the nature of the marketplace, such that organic is viewed as a premium product and can command much higher profit margins. From a service perspective, the ability to speak to a live customer service representative at any time represents a preferred attribute.

A great example of a commitment to be distinctive is In-N-Out Burger as illustrated in Figure 3.13.

SUPERIOR VALUE

Value is not just price. Perceived value is the combination of customers' perception of the time involved—how they feel about a transaction and the price paid.

Customers' perceived value generally has a lot to do with risk factors. Typical risks include customers' thoughts about:

- If I call, how much of a hassle will it be?
- How fast can I get in and out?
- Will the associates be friendly and helpful?
- Is the location convenient?
- Do the associates really care about how I feel?
- How long will the checkout lines be?
- What happens if I'm not satisfied?

It's therefore important when considering a promise that careful thought be given to how a promise can turn risk factors into preference factors, such as the fastest response or a guarantee that's real.

One successful retailer conducted in-store surveys that included 15 specific questions about its customers' shopping experience over the previous six months. Five of those questions focused on the customers' perception of the speed of various store experiences. It's obvious that they understood the importance of a perception of superior value related to customer's time involved.

In summary, a promise separates substance from hype. It's not a billboard, or about a presentation. It's the personal commitment that all the people in an organization make concerning how they want their customers to feel. The following brand profile of the RK Dixon Company illustrates how a nonconsumer business utilizes the right philosophy for success.

BRAND PROFILE

RK DIXON COMPANY

RK Dixon Company is a regional, family owned and operated business headquartered in Davenport, Iowa. It services customers in 79 counties in Iowa, Illinois, and Wisconsin. For over 20 years, it has built an enviable reputation as a result of its promise. With the help of Henry Russell Bruce (HRB), it reenergized its brand identity to more clearly communicate the promise of, "Everything just runs better."

RK Dixon has always believed that its customers should experience excellent service whether it involves a phone call, an e-mail, or a face-to-face meeting. Everything the company does is designed to make a difference in how its customers feel, whether it allows the customer to have a better day because they can talk to a real person, receive a faster response, or get their equipment up and running to get a job done.

It's all about creating pleasant experiences, and here are some of the ways they accomplish this:

- An employee (not an automated attendant) answers all calls coming into the offices. In an effort to reduce the number of calls placed on hold or transferred, the operations professionals are cross-trained to handle most of the incoming calls. Most of the calls fall into two areas—a supply order or a service call.
- When a customer places a supply order, it is immediately entered into RK Dixon's order processing

FIGURE 3.14

FIGURE 3.15

Everything just runs better®

---

system, and if it's received by 2:30 p.m., the order is shipped same day.

- Once a service call is placed, it is paged out to a technician, and the customer will receive a phone call from the assigned technician within two hours. The company is dedicated to exceptional response times. At the end of each call, the technician leaves a "customer care card" (mini satisfaction survey) which allows the customers to voice their opinion. All cards that are mailed in are reviewed daily and tracked. All concerns prompt an immediate call to the customer from the technician's manager. The company encourages the return of the satisfaction cards by offering the customer a chance to win a very nice dinner by entering their card into a drawing, and the technician listed on the call receives the same gift.

- Every month the company sends out surveys to randomly selected customers who have either called in for supplies or placed a service call. All the information received from the survey is tracked and reviewed by management to optimize a pleasant experience for every customer.

- On a monthly basis the operations group (anyone who answers the phone) attends classes to focus on improving customer service experiences as well as a variety of telephone skill topics. RK Dixon refers to this internally as "OnCourse to better Customer Service." The class sizes are small to encourage participation and to effectively keep the phone lines covered while classes are in session. Throughout the building, employees are reminded of customer service experiences with entertaining posters. A 15-minute follow-up is held every two weeks to gain insight on what is working and what is not. "Being one of the facilitators has been a great opportunity to listen to the ownership everyone takes when they answer a call. OnCourse has helped with not only our external customer service but internal as well," says Sue Hill, vice president of marketing.

- All service technicians and managers attended customized training meetings. In developing their customer service campaign, RK Dixon sought help from an outside expert. To gather information from the field, the expert traveled to branch locations with several technicians to experience every aspect of their work. This resulted in a customized program that was developed and implemented. In a group setting, topics included every aspect of a technician's visit, from how to greet with the proper handshake, convey the proper body language, and effectively communicate that the service visit was completed. Technicians went into the field with this new information and in 30 days convened in small work groups to provide feedback and suggest the best demonstrated practices. Continuous training is provided to managers, giving them the tools to continue the reinforcement of providing pleasant experiences.

The concept behind the "on button" graphic identity is to signal customers that when they call, RK Dixon is ready to deliver on their promise.

Bryan Dixon, president and CEO says that, "Everything just runs better" is not only our promise, it is how our employees think. They take ownership of the customer experience and want to help in every way they know how."

When new employees are hired, they spend a day at the corporate office for orientation. Part of that day consists of understanding every aspect of the business throughout the corporate office and of meeting colleagues.

Current employees are always ready to meet new employees and share how they deliver the RK Dixon promise of making everything run better. Once the introduction is finished, the current employees are asked, "How long have you been at RK Dixon?" They are proud to tout their number of years with the company and end the conversation with the comment: "I hope you enjoy working for the company as much as I do and here is my reason why ..."

Of RK Dixon employees, 53 percent have been there for five years or more. "At RK Dixon the employees are people who enjoy getting up each day and coming to work and that is the difference in having a promise and keeping it," says Bryan Dixon.

HOW LONG HAVE YOU BEEN AT RK DIXON?

"53% of RK Dixon's employees have been there for five or more years. At RK Dixon the employees are people who enjoy getting up each day and coming to work and that is the difference in having a promise and keeping it."

—Bryan Dixon

Used with permission.

THOUGHT GUIDE

THE ROADMAP TO A BRANDPROMISE COMMITMENT

- Functional excellence is a requirement for all genuine brands; long-term distinctiveness is based on the emotional side of the Brand Balance.
- An organization's promise should be developed around how it wants its customers to feel. Then it can decide what it should do to create the right experiences.
- Exceptional customer experiences can increase sales, profits, and shareholder value.
- In order to focus on the customer, an organization's traditional decision hierarchy may need to change.
- Most mergers, acquisitions, or corporate consolidations do not improve customer experiences.

- A brand needs to understand which attributes are "must haves" and those that "may" or "will" differentiate consumers' perceptions.
- Research should be used to create a brand "perceptual map" that focuses on four key areas. These insights become the foundation for developing an appropriate promise.
  - Distinctiveness
  - Relevance
  - Perceived value
  - Overall experience
- The better the promise, the better the brand experience for customers.
- Customer's perceived value of a particular brand is driven in part by "risk factors" such as the following for a retail experience:
  - If I call, how much of a hassle will it be?
  - How fast can I get in and out?
  - Will the associates be friendly and helpful?
  - Is the location convenient?
  - Do the associates really care about how I feel?
  - How long will the checkout lines be?
  - What happens if I'm not satisfied?

CHAPTER 4

Promises Are Delivered by People, Not Policies

Siding with the customer pays off for everyone in the end.[1]
—Jeff Bezos, founder of Amazon.com

PEOPLE ARE KEY

In Chapter 1, we introduced the three keys to success. One of these is the necessity for associates to feel that they are part of a brand's strategy and that they are passionate about delivering the promise. To be passionate about a promise is to believe in it and to desire to deliver it.

However, it seems as though many organizations are possessed by policy-mania, that is, having a policy to control every possible occurrence. Organizational policies are obviously important, but only to the extent necessary. A merchandise return policy cannot by itself create the desired customer emotional perception. Empowered associates make the difference in delivering a brand's promise.

One thing is for sure: if your organization, company, association, or nonprofit doesn't make a promise, then your associates may not know how they are supposed to make their customers or members feel.

FIGURE 4.1

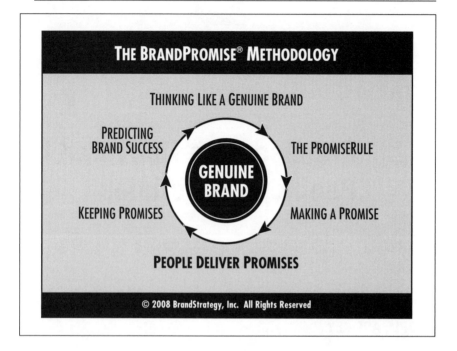

Too often, organizations that are involved in a branding or rebranding initiative never consider the internal training and culturalization implications. Unfortunately, the frontline associates who face the customers may be the last to know or understand their role in a new strategy. According to an article in *HR Magazine*, "An enterprise would be insane to conduct a massive external re-branding effort without finding a way to set the table internally, yet it seems to be a frequent situation."[2]

As Brad VanAuken, author of the *Brand Aid* book says, "The larger part of brand is how an organization delivers on its promise that really differentiates it from the rest of the marketplace."[3]

The traditional focus has been on products and services to create differentiation. However, the most important and sustainable differentiation may be how an organization's associates make its customers feel.

INTERNAL PROMISES

In certain situations, it seems that associates do not act as though they have a promise. They could be described as "placeholders," meaning that they are just there to be in that place, nothing more. Unfortunately, it seems as though placeholders are becoming more prevalent. It's common to approach a counter at an airport shop or a retail store or even a medical clinic and wait for the associates to finish a personal conversation. When the conversation is over, there isn't an apology, a greeting, or a warm smile, but rather the silent placeholder attitude that conveys, What do you want?

The natural question is: Whose fault is it? Let's assume that fault isn't important, but, really, why does this happen? If you ask placeholders, "What's their promise?" or "How do they want the customer to feel?" there's usually a blank stare.

FIGURE 4.2

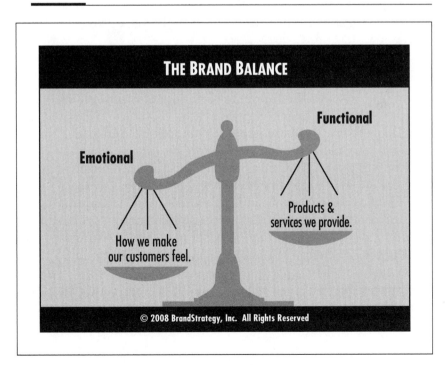

Why does this happen? Placeholders are the result of an organizational culture that has not embraced the importance of the Brand Balance (see Figure 4.2) related to making promises to customers or other associates.

Internal promises between associates and colleagues are just as important as external promises. An organization's "cultural trust" component may actually determine its ability to keep any kind of promises. Internal promises that are kept build a foundation for a brand's external promises. Associates' behaviors toward customers usually have a high correlation with their day-to-day interaction with management and other associates.

In the *Harvard Business Review* article titled "Promise Based Management (The Essence of Execution)," authors Donald Sull and Charles Spinosa outline the five characteristics of a good promise. Good promises are:

- Public (communicated publicly)
- Active (followed through in real time)
- Voluntary (associates want to make promises)
- Explicit (clear expectations)
- Mission-based (the rationale for a promise)[4]

"Promises are the fundamental units of interaction in businesses. They coordinate organizational activity and stoke the passions of employees, customers, suppliers, and other stakeholders."[5] "Leaders must, therefore, weave and manage their web of promises with great care, encouraging iterative conversation to make sure commitments are fulfilled reliably."[6]

In the book *BrandMindset*, we devoted a chapter to the importance of internalizing an organization's promise. We termed this *Brand Culturalization*. As Tina Goodwin writes in *Marketing News*, "Brand the customer relationship from the inside out. In many cases, the effort starts from the inside out to ensure that employees understand the company's mission, brand and offerings in order to best manage customer interactions."[7]

ENGAGING EXPERIENCES

One day when I was at Nordstrom's downtown Seattle store, I decided to try to get a quick lunch at the café even though it was very busy. I sat at the counter and ordered a salad and a brevè latte. A pleasant associate was quick to see that I was in a hurry but told me that the café did not have lattes. Before I could even consider my disappointment, he said, "If it's ok with you, I'll run upstairs and get you one from the outside e-bar cart." I was thrilled—and not prepared for his promise. He reappeared in about four minutes with the latte in a china cup and saucer, which he had brought with him to the cart, and my salad. The latte was perfect, and the Cobb salad exceptional. He was not following a policy; he was delivering the Nordstrom promise of outstanding customer service. Customer service has always been Nordstrom's number one goal, and the company works hard at making customers happy every day.

I had the pleasure of visiting the Ginn Reunion Resort in the Orlando, Florida, area. In all my encounters with dozens of associates at all levels, I never met a *placeholder*. How does this happen? Orlando's growth makes it one of the toughest labor markets in the United States. But still, how does it get associates who are passionate about the guest's experience? They recruit and hire associates who understand that how the guest feels is key.

This is not to suggest that policies are not essential in the operation of any successful organization. However, policies are all too often relied upon *in place* of a promise. A customer service policy, a return policy, or a "no more than three customers" in line policy may not achieve the desired customer feelings by themselves.

It's important that an organization's executive team understands this; however, the challenges are illustrated in Figure 4.3. Strativity Group, Inc., conducted an Internet survey of over 300 executives in the United States, Asia, Europe, and Africa that was published in *Marketing News*.[8] The results of this survey clearly indicate the lack of executive knowledge related to some of the most important "need to know" business information.

FIGURE 4.3

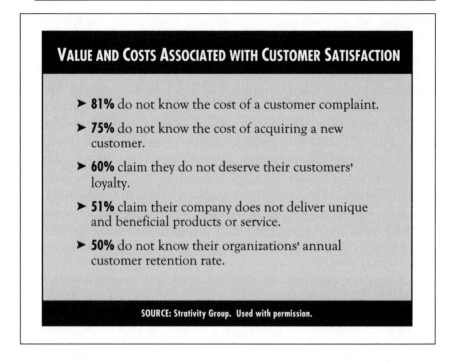

VALUE AND COSTS ASSOCIATED WITH CUSTOMER SATISFACTION

➤ **81%** do not know the cost of a customer complaint.

➤ **75%** do not know the cost of acquiring a new customer.

➤ **60%** claim they do not deserve their customers' loyalty.

➤ **51%** claim their company does not deliver unique and beneficial products or service.

➤ **50%** do not know their organizations' annual customer retention rate.

SOURCE: Strativity Group. Used with permission.

If senior executives do not understand the value and costs associated with customer satisfaction, it's a sure bet that they do not realize the importance of making a promise.

Unless everyone in an organization understands, agrees, and buys into a promise, then its brand can be at risk. More importantly, an organization's promise needs to become the associates' promise. Associates need to feel that they are part of any promise or strategic process, and they need to see an organization's leadership set examples and behave consistently with the promise.

John Yokoyama, owner of Pike Place Fish in Seattle's Pike Place Market, describes his "principles of power." "It says that basically you're it, you are the whole thing. It's the power of personal responsibility, meaning that you're willing to look at things from the point of view that you are personally responsible for your own experience of the world. It means to operate in your job as if you are the source of what is happening. It's based

FIGURE 4.4

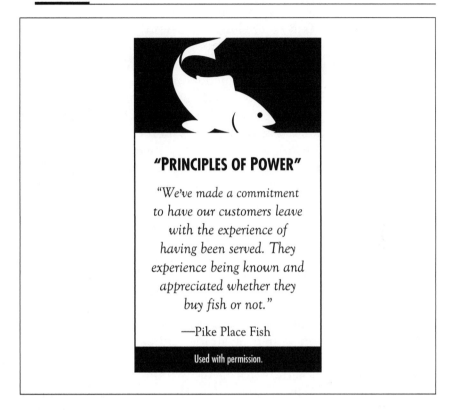

"PRINCIPLES OF POWER"

*"We've made a commitment
to have our customers leave
with the experience of
having been served. They
experience being known and
appreciated whether they
buy fish or not."*

—Pike Place Fish

Used with permission.

on the insight that groups of people don't create, only individuals create; but the point is that only individuals have the power to choose."[9]

THE BOARD'S RESPONSIBILITY

Corporate governance discussions have been the rage over the past few years resulting from the Sarbanes-Oxley legislation. As a result of this legislation and increased corporate scrutiny, major universities and large consulting firms are offering corporate governance retreats, symposiums, and audits focusing on financial reporting requirements, policies, ethics, and professional judgment. Accountability is the new mandate.

Most surprising is the lack of attention or even an understanding of the customer experience. Leading experts such as Peter Drucker and Tom Peters have consistently advised that companies be focused on their customers first. The Sarbanes-Oxley legislation is all about corporate directors exercising their independence to really know what's going on in their companies and ensuring that the appropriate policies and systems are in place.

Think about a company or industry that's failing, and most likely the consumers' experience has deteriorated and their perceptions of the company or industry have declined accordingly. While boards of directors have an important responsibility to be financially informed, many boards are out of touch with consumers' experiences and perceptions of their companies and brands.

According to John Gardner at Heidrick & Struggles, "The best in-class board fosters a culture of rigorous, relentless examination. It presses for continual improvement ... that reverberates throughout the organization to employees, customers and shareholders."[10]

It's clear from the major brand failures and corporate scandals that their management systems and safeguards were not working. The typical corporate financial reporting systems and traditional board practices are severely hampered by historic or backward-focused information. It's like trying to drive a car by looking in the rearview mirror. Executives and boards of directors who have focused too much attention on quarterly earnings, stock options, and enormous compensation plans have not built genuine brands.

The key to any company's success lies in its customers', consumers', associates', and influencers' perceptions and management's ability to understand and anticipate their needs and desires. All these stakeholders ultimately determine whether brands and companies are successful. A very effective way to monitor an organization's future is to understand how the business is perceived by its customers, consumers (distributors, retailers, franchisees, etc.), and associates.

While most companies would never consider "running the business" without monthly financials and independent audits, key strategic decisions are made regularly without an independent, consistent, strategic audit of consumers' and other stakeholders' perceptions. Our research shows that many of the recent corporate failures were really caused by "brand failure," which created the necessity for fictitious or questionable financial reporting. Even more surprising is that their boards of directors could have been "early warned" by an independent brand audit. A brand audit allows a board of any organization to think "outside in" (from the customer's perspective) as opposed to "inside out."

A McKinsey survey of more than 1,000 directors concluded that 70 percent of the directors wanted to know more about customers, competitors, suppliers, the likes and dislikes of consumers, market share, brand strength, levels of satisfaction with products, and so forth.[11]

Imagine every board of directors' meeting beginning with an independent brand audit that outlines customers', consumers', associates', and influencers' perceptions of key brand attributes such as distinctiveness, relevance, quality, perceived value, and the brand experience trend compared to competitors. Once again, a brand's success is based on how the internal stakeholders (employees, distributors, franchisees, or retailers) make their customers, consumers, associates, and influencers feel.

Dave Ulrich and Norm Smallwood's article in the July–August 2007 issue of *Harvard Business Review* suggests the importance of the customer's perspective at the board of directors' level: "One way to assess leaders' behavior through a customer lens is to open up feedback sessions to customers. A board of directors charged with evaluating the CEO recently went a couple of steps further, by asking not only customers but also investors and community leaders to comment on the actions and accomplishments of the CEO. Through this review, the CEO learned that he was not spending adequate time connecting with community leaders and with some segments of customers."[12]

To build a leadership brand, firms should assess leaders from the customer's point of view. One way to do that is to open up feedback sessions to customers.

—Dave Ulrich and Norm Smallwood, "Building a Leadership Brand," *Harvard Business Review,* July–August 2007

An organization's board of directors is ultimately responsible for their brand's success or failure and its effect on shareholder value. It is the board's responsibility to protect the most valuable corporate asset—the brand.

The traditional board focus on earnings has not always produced the right kind of company culture. I've heard CEOs say, "If sales are strong, I don't have to worry about consumers." This old-fashioned thinking resulted in the decline of many large corporations that were once the so-called leaders.

The new paradigm for boards demands that they truly understand how the enterprise's customers and consumers really feel. Only then can the right strategy be executed that produces exceptional brand experiences and increased shareholder value.

Consumers drive earnings and growth, not corporate CEOs. A poll of 1,400 CEOs of small and midsized companies by TEC International reported on the CEOs' short-term objectives. Number one on CEOs' list of "must-dos" to grow their companies in the next six months was to "reposition."[13] Successful strategies to reposition companies must be based on their customers', consumers', associates,' and influencers' perceptions of their brand, not a new advertising slogan.

If people deliver an organization's promise, it's essential for a board of directors to make the customers' experience the number one priority. In fact, I would argue that if a board doesn't take responsibility for the promise and the customer experience, then quite possibly no one else will either.

CREATING A PARADIGM SHIFT

After an organization has decided to make a promise, the next step is to develop an implementation plan to enable the organization to deliver its promise. We term this a "paradigm shift" mindset because transformation embodies the spirit of real change that's necessary for a corporation, nonprofit, association, and other types of organizations to become a genuine brand.

A paradigm shift is not about changing one aspect of a customer's experience, such as a product innovation involving a new package or flavor. It is about examining all of a brand's

FIGURE 4.5

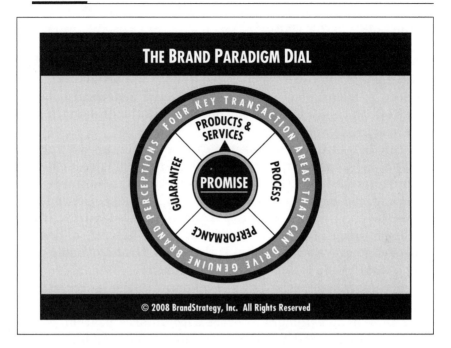

transactions with its customers, whether they are under the brand's direct control or not. The goal of a paradigm shift is to effect a fundamental change in a brand's strategic model that enhances its success as well as its perceived distinctiveness. Figure 4.5 outlines the four key transaction areas that can drive genuine brand perceptions among customers, consumers, associates, and influencers. These are the drivers used to create a paradigm shift in a brand's experience with its stakeholders.

The first driver is focused on products and services. As we mentioned before, product or service innovations frequently become the focus of a rebranding exercise. Michael Treacy, cofounder of GEN3 Partners, Inc., says, "Brand is a compact statement of the value proposition of a product. But the mere additions of flavors, scents, sizes, and other line extensions is not innovation."[14]

The question should always be, how can product and service innovations deliver on a promise and enhance customers' perceived value of a brand? Innovation can play a key role in developing a paradigm shift, but always as it relates to how an organization wants its customers to feel and not just in a product and service context.

Moving the dial in a clockwise direction, process becomes the second determinate. The process that an organization makes its customers endure may in fact be more important than the product. A friend of mine recently selected a new automobile over his first choice because the operation of the dashboard controls was too complicated.

Another example of the importance of the process relates to a call to a customer service center. After what seemed like 20 prompts and three different menus and ten minutes, the recording told me the offices were closed. This experience illustrates the point that regardless of the high-tech features, if the customer process is not fast, friendly, and helpful, it doesn't matter. Imagine how successful Alexander Graham Bell's telephone would have been without "operators."

A comprehensive analysis of an organization's processes is required before one can effectively transform and deliver a promise. When customers interact with an organization, is it a fast, convenient, and positive experience that enhances their perception of the brand?

The third key area affecting a paradigm shift is how our organization performs in the customer's mind. As a follow-up to the cell phone example we mentioned earlier, when I finally did get in touch with a customer service representative, how did they make me feel? There was no apology for the inconvenience or any other expression of care or concern. In fact, the representative seemed in a hurry to get the conversation over with. While the technical problem was ultimately resolved, the process and performance did not enhance my perception of the brand.

If you are reading this and wondering how you can instill the performance motivation throughout your organization, one answer is easy—change all your bonus plans so that at least 50 percent of all incentives are paid out only when customer service ratings for excellent and good scores reach a predetermined level.

Just to be clear, when we're talking about performance, it's not just about frontline, online, or telephone service; it's every aspect of how your associates make everyone feel—customers, colleagues, and so on.

The guarantee is the fourth driver for creating a paradigm shift and the importance of the right guarantee was detailed in Chapter 2. It's important to note that the right guarantee can really change the competitive landscape in your favor because it can serve as a powerful signal to your associates and customers that you have a promise.

Our extensive study of retailers indicates that while an organization may actually have an appropriate guarantee policy, it still may not be effectively executed by associates. All too often, we have observed situations in which associates feel that it is their job to determine who should get the guarantee. In other words, an organization's culture must consistently support and reward associates for honoring the guarantee. Human nature being as it is may produce judgmental behavior, even in the best of circumstances.

TRANSFORMATION

We define *transformation* as the "state of being changed in the form, appearance, nature, or character of an organization." When an organization makes a promise, the goal is to transform the entire entity to deliver its promise.

When Howard Schultz began building Starbucks around the promise of the "third place," it required a transformation mindset to deliver this promise of a place where people would feel welcome and be able to relax and indulge themselves. At that time, there were many other large worldwide coffee brands, and some people wondered why those brands didn't innovate to compete. Innovation is one part of transformation; however, when an experience is involved, it's not just about having lattes but about creating a paradigm shift in how you want your customers to feel.

In fact, once an organization makes a promise, there are usually hundreds of actions that have to be taken to actually deliver on the promise. These actions across the organization became the foundation for transformation.

According to Accenture Consulting, "Many companies wait too long to attempt transformations, doing so only when the signs of trouble have become obvious. But in today's unforgiving business environment, that's probably too late. High performers, by contrast, change before they must, knowing that the best way to transform is from a position of strength."[15]

Kathy Bell, vice president of Emerson Electric Co., explains, "It's really about delivering on promises, about being there for the customers."[16]

The promise doesn't end at the sale; it should be a lifelong commitment. "The mantra innovate or die stands as imperative, one that doesn't instantly snap into place with a companywide email."[17]

Successful transformations may be most applicable to existing organizations, companies, or nonprofits that have actually transformed themselves from one form to another. Examples would include Dayton Hudson's transformation to Target and Walton's Five and Dime to Wal-Mart. However, transformation can apply to a new entity if in fact that organization has changed the form, appearance, nature, or character of an industry or created a completely new form. Many other new transformations come to mind including FedEx, Amazon.com, and Microsoft.

Transforming within an existing entity is arguably more difficult than starting with something new. Hence, the transformation of Dayton Hudson into Target is a great study in how to

FIGURE 4.6

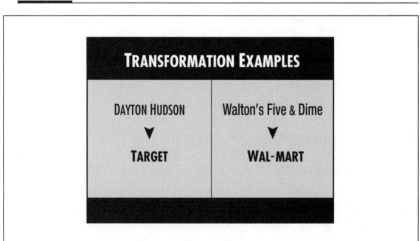

TRANSFORMATION EXAMPLES	
DAYTON HUDSON	Walton's Five & Dime
▼	▼
TARGET	WAL-MART

transform successfully. The Dayton Dry Goods store was founded in 1903 and became the Dayton Company in 1911. According to *Discount Store News*, in 1960, Dayton began to examine new retailing concepts and changing consumers' desires. Executives recommended a transformation concept based in part on a University of Denver research report. They wanted to develop a new retail concept—an upscale discount store.[18]

The company appointed two senior executives, Douglas J. Dayton and John Geisse, who assembled a team to develop the new retail model over the next 18 months. Dayton's proposed venture didn't follow the concept of other discounters, which focused on low-priced goods with seconds and irregulars as part of the mix. Dayton said, "We will offer high-quality merchandise at low margins, because we are cutting expenses. We would much rather do this than trumpet dramatic price cuts on cheap merchandise."[19]

"Dayton married its department store heritage and Geisse's insights to launch Target as the first upscale discounter, featuring an attractive shopping environment, an innovative racetrack layout, and a mix of products that included higher-priced merchandise."[20]

With its chain orientation, Target's merchandising and operating decisions were made at headquarters rather than at the individual stores, which is what most discounters were doing.

More than 200 names were considered for the new business, but none included the word "Dayton" so consumers wouldn't associate the new chain with the department store.[21]

The first Target store opened in May 1962, the first Kmart opened two months earlier, and the first Wal-Mart opened a few months later. Between 1962 and 1968, Target opened nine stores. Dayton's executives were uncertain about Target's viability because the discounter at first lost money.[22] It would appear that the Target stores were being hampered by Dayton's operating policies and a lack of experience in creating a new retail paradigm shift. Target's executives decided they needed to be separated from the parent company and move to separate offices.

In 1974, a two-year "remake" of Target began with an executive retreat. Company executives met at a nearby hotel for a week to develop Decision Guides—the operating policies and philosophies for the chain's future growth.[23]

The new strategy paid off. Target became the number one revenue producer for the Dayton Hudson Corporation in 1975. A third-generation new Target store prototype was unveiled in 1985. In 2000, Dayton Hudson changed its corporate name to Target Corporation.

Target Transformation Insights

- Target has been brand-savvy and uses "design" and style as brand requirements for everything it does, not just products.
- Target operates support services as "stand-alone" subsidiaries, such as private label, forensic security, and commercial interiors.
- Target's customer base tends to be younger, more educated, and affluent than discount competitors.
- Consumers have their own descriptor for Target's unique style by calling it "Tar-shay."
- Target makes a strong philanthropic promise; it is a leading corporate contributor in the United States (percentage of income compared to donations).
- Target pioneered "two-tier" brand messaging: style and image advertising are separate from discount and value circulars.

It's important to remember that transformation isn't a "once and done" but rather a major paradigm shift followed by a continuous reevaluation and migration of your "best practices" as outlined in Figure 4.7. Transformation should always be focused on how an organization wants customers, consumers, associates, and influencers to feel and then create the right products, services, process, performance, and guarantee to ensure exceptional brand perceptions.

In many cases, successful transformations of existing organizations have included a separate chief executive officer and an independent operating entity to escape the "parent entity's" old ideas. The goal is to think about customers and markets in nontraditional ways. Keep in mind that most transformations underperform in their early stages.

FIGURE 4.7

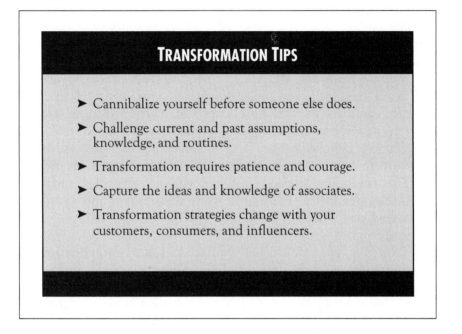

It's always important to focus on creating distinctive functional and emotional perceptions in the minds of your target audience. Here are four keys to transformation success. Focus on:

- Simpler, easy-to-use applications
- More convenient accessibility
- Higher perceived value and valued solutions
- Emotionally stimulating messages

Successful brands embrace the promise philosophy. The following brand profile of Bartell Hotels demonstrates this principle.

BRAND PROFILE
_____

BARTELL HOTELS

One of the keys to making and keeping a promise is the CEO's passion for the commitment that's required.

When I first met Richard Bartell, the chief executive officer of Bartell Hotels, I was most impressed with the fact that he actually read the various hotel comment cards from guests. He was genuinely concerned about the guests' experience.

Bartell Hotels is the largest independently owned hotel company in San Diego with seven different properties including The Dana on Mission Bay, as well as several franchised hotels. Several of the hotels are quite distinctive, and even the franchised properties consistently receive exceptional customer service recognition.

However, Bartell Hotels wanted to take its dedication to excellence to the next level. All the key executives, including the director of sales for each property, worked extensively over several months to complete a Brand Assessment and then to develop a promise. They proactively interviewed many employees and also benefited from guests suggestions.

FIGURE 4.8
_____

Used with permission.

Bartell Hotels' promise is illustrated in Figure 4.9 and focuses on, "Relax and Enjoy! Great Day. Every Day!"

As we have discussed before, the promise is not necessarily the advertising message, but it should drive the spirit and essence of all communications. Richard Bartell explains, "Every employee plays a critical role in exceeding our guests' expectations. We spent as much time talking about how we wanted our employees to feel as we did about how we wanted our guests to feel. We wanted to develop within each employee a sense of purpose with a mission. We felt it was vital for our employees to

FIGURE 4.9

Used with permission.

FIGURE 4.10

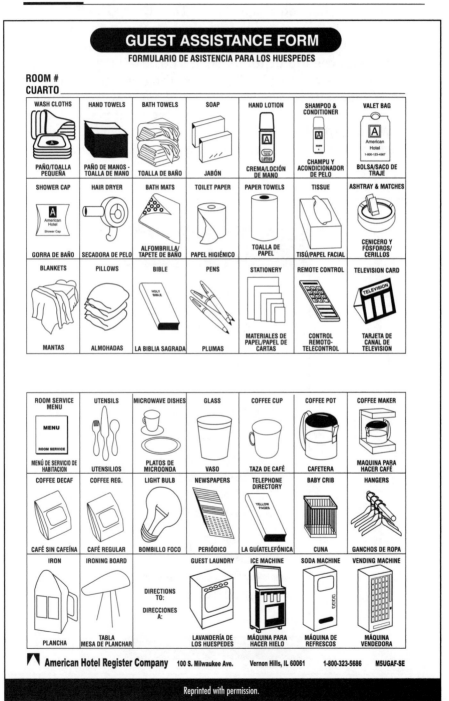

truly *want* to exceed our guests' expectations and to feel empowered to do so. Our focus became how to instill that desire and empowerment in our staff. The way they communicate our promise to the guest is as important as the promise itself."

During the development of the promise, the Bartell team's mindset related to defining "Bartell's job" and the "guests' job" was very effective in focusing on the benefits for the guests and not the process. Of course, the key to success is not just making a promise, but living it. The Bartell team created a long list of action steps, which are critical to bringing a promise to life. One of their most interesting action steps was to empower every employee to grant an act of kindness to any guest. Employees are provided with small paper scrolls, which can be presented to the guest. The scrolls are "surprise acts of kindness" and are all about providing "special moments" for the guests. Guests then receive a special thank you. As an example, guests could receive an in-room amenity, an upgrade to a suite, or a free appetizer or dessert.

Another idea was to address potential language challenges between employees and guests. The Dana Hotel began using the guest assistance form shown in Figure 4.10. Every employee can carry this guide to help when communications can benefit from a picture as well as words. Most importantly, an action step like this makes an enormous impact on employees' confidence and self-assurance and, of course, it makes guests feel great too.

THOUGHT GUIDE

PROMISES ARE DELIVERED BY PEOPLE, NOT POLICIES

- Promises should be delivered by people and not be the result of policies; hence, every associate is an ambassador for the brand.
- Placeholders are associates who do not understand a brand's promise or choose not to deliver the promise to customers. Everyone in an organization should understand, agree on, and buy into the promise.
- Internal promises among executives, managers, and associates are just as important as external promises to customers. Associates' behavior toward customers is linked to associates' interactions with a brand's managers and executives.

- When associates take personal responsibility for creating the right customer experience, a brand's promise comes alive.
- Customers and associates ultimately determine whether brands are successful over the long term.
- Boards of directors require financial audits, and they should also conduct independent brand audits of the organization's promise.
- In order to become a genuine brand, many organizations must transform their appearance, nature, or character in order to deliver their promise.
- A promise doesn't end at the sale of a product or service. It continues with every thought or experience that customers have concerning a brand.
- It's important to understand that a brand transformation isn't a "once and done" exercise, but rather a major paradigm shift that occurs over time.
- Transformation tips:
  - Cannibalize yourself before someone else does.
  - Challenge current and past assumptions, knowledge, and routines.
  - Transformation requires patience and courage.
  - Capture the ideas and knowledge of associates.
- Transformation strategies must change over time in order to be relevant with customers, consumers, and influencers.
- Transformation is all about making a customer's experience easier by creating:
  - Simpler, easy-to-use applications
  - More convenient accessibility
  - Higher perceived value and valued solutions
  - Emotionally stimulating messages

Five Ways to Keep Promises

The difficulty lies not so much in developing new ideas as in escaping the old ones.

—John Maynard Keynes

KEEPING PROMISES

The idea of keeping promises is fundamental to the BrandPromise methodology. It's important to acknowledge that it's not always easy, but what could be more important?

Imagine how different things would be if publicly held companies voluntarily released their quarterly earnings with an independent report of their customer satisfaction scores. How about executive compensation plans that require exceptional customer satisfaction levels in order for workers to receive a bonus or stock-related benefits?

These may seem like wild ideas. However, the paradigm shifts caused by eBay, Amazon.com, and others have occurred because consumers wanted a "better way" to shop. In fact, prior to the beginning of the Internet retail craze, research indicated that over 75 percent of consumers wanted a better way to shop. Consumers love to be able to see whether sellers keep their promises before they buy in the new online world. Recent history

FIGURE 5.1

THE BRANDPROMISE® METHODOLOGY

THINKING LIKE A GENUINE BRAND

PREDICTING
BRAND SUCCESS

THE PROMISERULE

GENUINE
BRAND

KEEPING
PROMISES

MAKING A PROMISE

PEOPLE DELIVER PROMISES

© 2008 BrandStrategy, Inc. All Rights Reserved

clearly confirms that new and better customer experiences can quickly achieve an increased share of consumers' wallets.

MAKE A PROMISE!

▼

The companies and organizations you can trust make a PROMISE and keep it!

WHOM CAN YOU TRUST?

Ask your friends to share their recent exceptional experiences as a customer, and it's easy to understand why trust may not be the first thing that springs to mind when consumers think of certain products and services in the market place.

You can trust the companies and organizations that make a promise and keep it. The goal of any organization should be to enhance its customers' lives. Our basic system of free enterprise was founded on trust. If companies are providing a product or service, consumers should be able to trust that they're going to deliver that product or service with the consumers' best interests in mind. Genuine brands need to be perceived as distinctive or one of a kind. With many examples of broken promises in the news every day, there is an enormous opportunity to stand out by the nature of a genuine promise.

"If a company can create and deliver on a clear promise, consumers will reward them with business and loyalty," says communications and management consultant Lorne Daniel of Grandview Consulting. Daniel, who led a brand plan initiative for one of Canada's leading optometry groups, Doctors Eyecare Network, says, "A strong promise can really distinguish a brand by delivering tangible benefits for both consumers and organizations."

In 2007, MSN Money introduced its Customer Service Hall of Shame and ranked the 10 worst customer service companies according to 3,000 respondents. The top 10 worst rated included several large banks, telecommunications brands, and cable TV companies. What's most interesting is that telecommunication and cable companies want to become consumers' single source for telephone, Internet, and cable TV services. If a brand provides exceptional customer experiences and keeps its promises, it can avoid this kind of negative publicity.

Let's look at some everyday examples of why keeping promises is so important.

FRUSTRATING EXPERIENCES

Incentives are supposed to make customers feel good about a brand, not feel cheated or angry. Incentives such as rebates, rain checks, frequent-flyer miles, or points that are difficult or impossible to redeem may not be a wise strategy.

Example: Rebates

How many times have you looked at an ad on the Internet or in a store and thought, "Oh, great, only $199"—or whatever the price? And then you look more carefully; that price would be the total after you've received one or two rebates. So you think, well, okay. So it's $240 now, but then the rebate check will come and you'll feel like you've saved. So you buy the item.

Then you get it home and unpack it and start to try to figure out the rebate scheme. You may have to go retrieve the box from the trash to cut out the bar code. Then you have to remember where you put the receipt, or receipts, depending on the exact rebate format you have, and then you have to copy everything, for your records, of course, and send to the rebate company only the originals, according to the exact rules. Then you wait. If you are lucky, a check will arrive some time in the future. If you are unlucky, the check will roll in months late or not at all—the issuing business has gone bankrupt. Or a letter will arrive saying, in various ways, that the forms you sent in were not correct and now the deadline for rebate fulfillment is past. Too bad.

Many consumers' reaction when they see or hear the word "rebate" is an instant feeling of avoidance: I don't do rebates after realizing how the system works. The only rebate I ever received was the result of sending the paperwork by certified, return receipt mail, and then it took four months. Recently, I observed a customer at an office superstore who asked the checkout employee about a rebate: "Why don't they just charge us $50 less?" The checkout employee giggled and said, "They expect you to forget. That's how they make their money!" The employee, acknowledging the complexity of the rebate system, helpfully offered assistance in filling out the rebate forms then and there.

According to a *Mercury News* article, roughly 40 percent of people actually send in their rebate forms. "Let's say a manufacturer expects to sell 100,000 units of an item that sells for $899 and offers a $100 rebate. The manufacturer is banking on a 60 percent redemption rate, so the cost of the rebate program would be an expected $6 million. But if everyone correctly applied for the rebates or if the company simply cut the price by $100, the cost to the company would be $10 million."[1] It's easy to see why companies find rebates appealing.

A research project by consulting firm Vericours, Inc., confirmed that about 40 percent of rebate offers are never redeemed, which amounts to some $10 billion in unpaid rebates.[2] Fifty or a hundred bucks here or there may seem like a forgettable amount to an individual. But multiply that amount by many thousands and that adds up to serious money for a company.

You can find rants from bloggers throughout the Internet describing their long and fruitless attempts to get rebate checks. Some will say that the company claims it never received the customer's papers, or that they were improperly filled out, or that the check is in the mail—all claims that customers and time disprove. But companies may not get away with this "theft by omission" for long. According to some state laws, after three years, checks issued but not cashed belong to the state.

Consumers, too, are getting wise. According to the *AARP Bulletin*, the Better Business Bureau reports that complaints about rebates have soared by 400 percent since 2002.[3] The Federal Trade Commission (FTC) reports that most rebates go unclaimed because rules are too complicated or vague. The FTC, in 2005, ruled that one company had engaged in "deceptive trade practices" and ordered it to pay up, not only on its own products for which rebate promises had not been fulfilled, but on the products of one of its suppliers, which had gone bankrupt, leaving rebates unpaid.[4]

Complex rebate policies can end up being expensive for companies. One electronics company, whose rebate policy stipulated that only one rebate could be recognized per address, failed to take into consideration apartment buildings, so hundreds of rebate holders were denied. In a settlement in a New York court, it was ordered to pay $200,000 in rebates to some 4,000 customers.[5]

Because of customer complaints, several large retailers are considering or actually have discontinued mail-in rebates. Instead they offer rebates at the checkout counter.

Lesson

For retailers, the best way to keep customers coming back is not to make them mad. Consumers have many choices. For manufacturers, rebates may make sense, but if a company is going to offer them, then it should honor them—and make it fast and easy. The last thing you would want is to make people mad as they're unpacking and setting up their new item, which has your name all over the box.

THE BEST PART

▼

Make the communication process with your customers the BEST part of their experience!

Example: Telephone Call Centers

Make the communication process with customers the best part of their experience, not the worst part. If an organization doesn't want to talk with customers, then it shouldn't offer customer service or not have voice mail. This would be much wiser than a voice-mail system with dozens of prompts and long wait times which create consumer contempt.

Another frequent frustration is a conversation with a customer service representative that does not solve the problem. The consumer asks for the company's headquarters phone number, and the response is; "I can't give that information out," or, "I don't know."

I received a letter from a large company that had emerged from bankruptcy. The letter described how things were going to be much better. The next weekend, I called the customer service center and hung up after 30 minutes on hold. The next day the wait was 45 minutes before finally reaching a live representative.

Lesson

The president and chief executive officer of any organization should personally experience, on a weekly basis, how customers are treated in the three most frequent transactions: online, telephone, and in person.

- Call the customer call center once a week at the busiest time and try to purchase a product or service. Then try to return it or get a refund.
- If customer service cannot answer calls in three to five minutes, then customers should be told how long they can expect to wait.
- Visit offices or retail stores and observe customer experiences. Are they exceptional?

WHAT'S FAIR?

Always treat customers better than they expect to be treated, and always be fair.

Example: Credit Card Refunds and Warranties

Credit Card Charges

When customers purchase an item on a credit card, the amount is posted almost immediately to their account. When customers return a purchase, the credit should appear on their account just as fast—not weeks or months later, or as they love to say, "the next billing cycle."

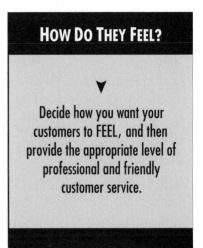

HOW DO THEY FEEL?

▼

Decide how you want your customers to FEEL, and then provide the appropriate level of professional and friendly customer service.

Extended Warranties

Extended warranties have become big business for retailers. However, there is some question as to whether some may lead to long-term consumer satisfaction.

"There appears to be a growing awareness that these are a sucker's bet," said Tod Marks, a senior editor at *Consumer Reports* magazine. "The best idea is to take the money you would have spent on a warranty and put it in the bank," says Marks.[6] Retailers push multiyear warranties aggressively because they're a huge source of profit. Stores keep 40 to 50 percent of what they charge for warranties, according to *Warranty Week*, a trade newsletter. Only about 20 percent goes toward repairs.[7]

Extended warranties can provide peace of mind, and many provide a valued service and a positive experience. It's important to compare the cost to the probability of repair within the time frame covered and the difficulty involved in actually receiving the warranty benefit.

Home Warranties

When buying a resale home, the prospect of a home warranty may be a good idea. Not having to worry about repairs for a year sounds enticing, and warranties can be very helpful in completing the sale of a home.

However, here's the reality check. The servicing company is usually not a local firm. Let's say that someone purchases a home only to find out that the hot-water tank is not working. The homeowner must contact a centralized call center to report the problem. If it's a weekend or the home is outside a metropolitan area, it may take several days for the warranty company's plumber to show up. If the customer gets frustrated and calls a local plumber, he or she will probably not be reimbursed for the new hot-water tank or the labor.

Lesson

Every organization that cares about its reputation should be regularly asking the question: Are the products and services we are selling (especially those that are provided by a third party) providing real value and exceptional experiences to our customers?

THE RIGHT PROMISE IS KEY

The good news is that organizations that choose to make a *genuine* promise to their customers can create an opportunity to be truly distinctive.

There are five key rules that organizations can apply to avoid breaking promises to customers and losing their trust:

1. Always make customers feel *appreciated* and *cared about* when they have a problem or need help, not just when they make a purchase.
2. Make your organization's number one goal to have the *happiest customers,* not to be the biggest or fastest growing company around.
3. When an organization begins to anticipate a merger, acquisition, consolidation, downsizing, or other type of

corporate transaction, *focus on keeping customers happy first* and the necessary business details second.

4. *Measure, recognize,* and *reward* the associates who actually delight your customers. Focus on how your associates make your customers feel and not whether they just answer the phone or do their daily job.

5. Develop and commit to a customer *bill of rights.* Make it fundamental to your organization's culture and not just policy.

FIGURE 5.2

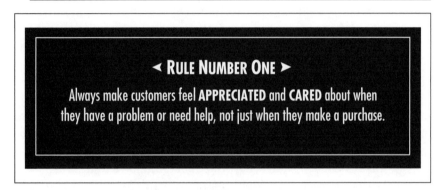

◄ RULE NUMBER ONE ►

Always make customers feel **APPRECIATED** and **CARED** about when they have a problem or need help, not just when they make a purchase.

Most successful companies make customers feel good when they purchase a product or service. However, when customers call for help or a refund after a purchase of a product or service, are they made to feel just as good as, or even better than, when they made the purchase?

When consumers call a catalog company to purchase a product, they call toll-free, and someone always answers the call live! When the same consumers want customer service or need a refund or credit, in many cases the number is not toll-free, and the call is answered by an automated system. When they need customer service, do customers typically feel as good as, or better than, they did when they made the purchase? Is customer service usually as fast and friendly as the original purchase call?

Why not make "pleasant surprises" part of a promise strategy? Here are a few ideas to get the creative process started:

- Respond to inquiries, questions, requests, and so on within 24 hours of receiving them.
- Have a real person answer the phone.
- Make a follow-up call to ensure that the customer experience was good.
- Send a thank you note from a real person or a gift card for frequent purchases that the brand keeps track of.
- Deliver products earlier than expected.
- Provide free shipping for purchases and returns.

Think back to the last time you signed up for a new credit card. It was easy, fast, and probably painless, and the representative was friendly and eager to help. Is the service the same if your payment is late or if you have a problem with a bogus charge?

Many brands, including American Express, Costco, and Nordstrom, are focused on making the "customer service" experience just as positive as the original purchase.

A frequent practice in the mortgage business is for banks or other financial institutions to make home loans to their customers and then within a few months or a year sell that loan to a large mortgage servicing company. The customer's personal banker no longer has anything to do with that mortgage or the details.

Customers receive a form letter informing them of the new rules and procedures for making their payments. If they had a direct withdrawal payment, they may need to go through a completely new process. If they want to change the terms or other features of the loan, it will be quite a different experience from dealing with their personal banker.

FIGURE 5.3

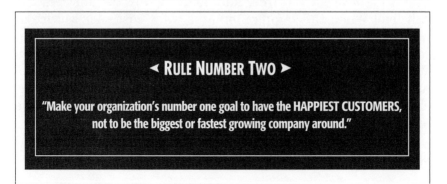

◄ RULE NUMBER TWO ►

"Make your organization's number one goal to have the HAPPIEST CUSTOMERS, not to be the biggest or fastest growing company around."

Financial institutions should be focused on making sure that their customers are delighted. Growth should not be a distraction from their primary focus—their customers.

One of the largest banks continues to advertise and tout its size and convenience. However, the fact is when customers present a check on their bank in another state or region, they are not treated like they are from the same bank. In one case, a customer wanted to pay off his mortgage by making payments from his checking account. He was forced to get a cashier's check and then send it to his bank's office in another state.

A common problem today with many big brands is that they have achieved their size through mergers and acquisitions, and their service is not seamless to their customers. In *Boardroom Briefing*'s issue on mergers and acquisitions, Graham Galloway and Dale Jones point out that, "There is a strategic promise behind every acquisition—and leadership has to be able to deliver on that promise."[8] While a company may represent and advertise that it is one brand, its customers have to deal with a collection of different organizations, cultures, and policies.

Whenever an organization touts its size or growth, the question should be asked: What's most important—how customers feel or how big the organization is?

The corporate landscape is littered with once great brands that ruined their customers' experiences, as well as their success, in the name of growth or greed.

FIGURE 5.4

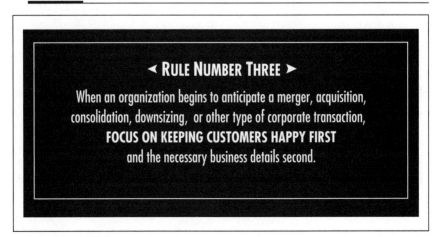

One of the most frequent mistakes companies make when a merger or acquisition takes place is that the new company changes the name of an acquired brand. Does anyone ever ask how the customers of Brand A will feel when they have enjoyed a long and trusted relationship only to wake up one morning to discover that Brand A is no more?

David Pinto analyzed this very issue in *Mass Market Retailers*, the global newspaper for supermarkets, drugstores, and discount stores. He advised, "Change the name of a favored, venerable or easily recognized retailer and you better have some good reasons."[9] Every time a retailer breaks this rule, it is always quick to point out the need for "one national advertising campaign," "operating cost savings," or, my favorite, "It will accelerate our growth plan."

"The name on the door of the acquiring company retailer inevitably appears to carry a glossier and more appealing cachet than that of the retailer being acquired."[10] The problem is that in many cases the customers not only dislike the new name, but the new operations, policies, procedures, and customer service that came with the change. This is not to say that one larger brand name does not have its advantages, but only if the customers perceive it to be an improvement.

Here are some guidelines for brand identity change involving a merger or acquisition. If an acquired brand has a positive reputation with its customers, make the brand identity change over a reasonable period of time. One option is to use both of the brands in advertising and internal and external communications. Earn customers' trust, and maintain or even enhance their positive experiences before the brand is changed.

We're not talking about being nice as some social experiment. If customers become disenchanted after a merger or name change, there's no amount of cost savings that can make up for the loss of sales or loyalty. The issue of customer service is not just a challenge for customers. Shareholders need to pay attention too. According to Joe Calloway, a customer service expert and author of *Work Like You're Showing Off*, "If you want to know how a company is doing, look at their sales. If you want to know how they are going to do in the future, look at their customer service. You can only tick people off for so long."[11]

FIGURE 5.5

People support that which they help to create. Associates who feel that they are involved in a brand's strategy and the development of policies and procedures are eager to please customers because they feel that it's their strategy.

The technological advances of e-mail, voice mail, and text messages may offer so-called convenient access but are not a substitute for a meeting of the minds and hearts. Because of time demands on everyone, customer policies and procedures easily become a process task characterized by a "get it done" and "move on" mentality. As the many previous examples of poor customer service indicate, customers' feelings are not receiving the kind of attention they deserve.

Time-starved consumers feel appreciated when organizations acknowledge their stress and respond in a timely manner. According to *USA Today*, a Yankelovich online survey of 1,349 consumers in 2006 indicated the following:

- 68 percent of time-starved people say they are likely to hang up if they're put on hold.
- 61 percent say they'll cancel an online purchase if processing takes too long.
- 56 percent say they'll walk out of a store immediately if the checkout lines are extremely long.[12]

Organizations that understand this time challenge are focused on making it easier for their customers by editing choices and saving valuable time. A popular and successful shoe retailer in a small town exemplifies this strategy. When customers can't find what they want, a specific brand or shoe in their store, the store goes online, finds the shoe, and orders it for the customers. While the store may not make its typical profit on the sale, customers perceive it as a "one stop shop," and their loyalty leads to the next sale.

Its' a constant battle to fit everything into a day. Hence, consumers' decisions on which brands to invite into their lives becomes an ever more difficult challenge. Individuals and organizations that make a distinctive promise based on real emotional and functional benefits are most likely to be the ones welcomed in.

One of Whole Foods' core values is, "We care about team member happiness and excellence." In a service environment, happy associates are the requirement if you expect to delight your customers; it's not optional. Enlightened organizations provide innovative compensation plans that reward employees for delighting customers and not just for showing up.

The critical question to ask is: If you expect to delight your customers, how will you delight your associates? You can't have one without the other.

It might seem like a good idea to have a customer bill of rights. But let's say that an organization is quite successful; why does it need one? Our analysis of hundreds of retailers,

FIGURE 5.6

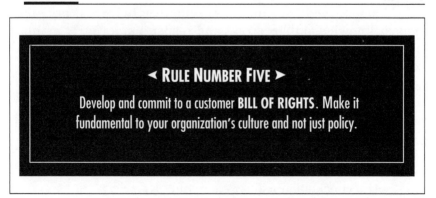

◄ RULE NUMBER FIVE ►

Develop and commit to a customer **BILL OF RIGHTS**. Make it fundamental to your organization's culture and not just policy.

health-care providers, hospitality brands, and restaurant brands consistently confirms that even in the best of cases associates tend to interpret and make their own rules over time.

In one example, a retailer utilized what seemed to be a very fair return policy. When we researched customer satisfaction, there seemed to be negative perceptions of the return policy. We discovered that despite the existence of a consumer-friendly return policy, it was not enhancing customer satisfaction. After interviewing a sampling of retail associates, it was clear that three things were happening.

1. Retail associates interpreted the policy based on their own feelings about customers.
2. The associate training program relied heavily on on-the-job training, and the return policy was not presented as a fundamental part of the brand's promise.
3. Store managers perceived the return policy as a negative as it related to their profit performance.

According to Don Butler, vice president of the National Retail Federation, "Sometimes associates can feel overprotective of company assets."[13] Hence, a customer-friendly return policy that is not proactive and reinforced may become detrimental to the company, because associates don't see the return policy as part of the brand experience. It is absolutely essential that an organization's values and promise be reinforced with associate behavior and enlightened policies that deliver the desired customer perceptions.

JetBlue Airways truly created a paradigm shift with its brand of service. However, regardless of how good a brand's service is, a crisis situation can change perceptions quickly. JetBlue experienced a crisis in 2007 when severe weather paralyzed its schedule. To the company's credit, it responded immediately with a customer bill of rights to let its customers know exactly what they could expect when things don't go as planned.

In an effort to protect its citizens, the city of Seattle instituted a cable customer bill of rights, which calls for cable employees to "be courteous, knowledgeable and helpful" and to "provide effective and satisfactory service in all contacts with customers."[14]

ENHANCING CUSTOMERS' EXPECTATIONS

A customer bill of rights makes it clear for everyone what an organization believes in. And it reinforces how it wants its customers to feel. More importantly, it also makes it clear to associates what is expected of them.

An appropriate customer bill of rights is a critical element in any strategy for a brand to truly become perceived as genuine and one of a kind. A customer bill of rights needs to provide specific benefits and be reinforced by the president, chief executive officer, or chairman.

A customer bill of rights should be a perfect extension of an organization's promise. It should outline certain expectations related to a promise. It also becomes a front-and-center communication strategy both internally and externally.

Evergreen Surgical Center, in Kirkland, Washington, is very committed to exceptional medical care. It has adopted a comprehensive Patient Bill of Rights. Here is a representative sample of its commitment to patients:

- Receive safe, private, high-quality, and respectful care.
- Have your comfort needs addressed.
- Know the name of your physician and others who care for you.
- Actively participate in decisions involving your care, including ethical issues, and be informed of any change in plan of care in advance.
- Receive care from personnel who are properly trained to perform assigned tasks and coordinate services.
- Courteous and respectful treatment of person and property, privacy, and freedom from abuse and discrimination.
- Access information in your own patient record upon request.
- Seek a second opinion or choose another caregiver.

A bill of rights can become a perfect brand signal for customers, and it can apply to any type of business, organization, or brand including health care and nonprofits. Figure 5.7 outlines the AutoSport catalog's customer bill of rights.

FIGURE 5.7

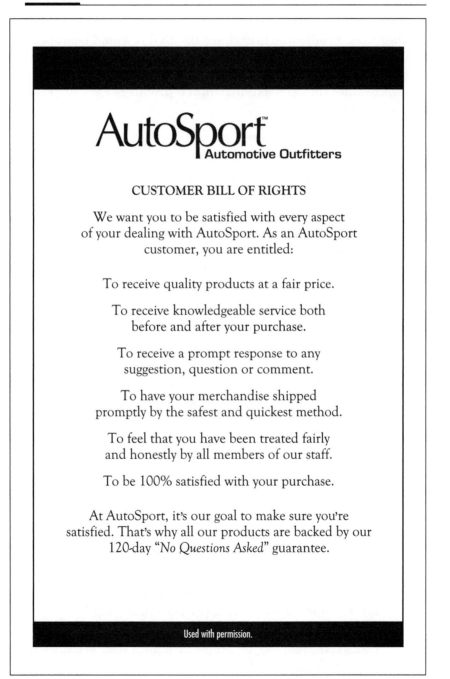

AutoSport™
Automotive Outfitters

CUSTOMER BILL OF RIGHTS

We want you to be satisfied with every aspect
of your dealing with AutoSport. As an AutoSport
customer, you are entitled:

To receive quality products at a fair price.

To receive knowledgeable service both
before and after your purchase.

To receive a prompt response to any
suggestion, question or comment.

To have your merchandise shipped
promptly by the safest and quickest method.

To feel that you have been treated fairly
and honestly by all members of our staff.

To be 100% satisfied with your purchase.

At AutoSport, it's our goal to make sure you're
satisfied. That's why all our products are backed by our
120-day "No Questions Asked" guarantee.

Used with permission.

BRAND PROFILE

Rather than profile one brand, we decided it would be appropriate to honor all the brands that are recognized by independent organizations for their excellence. There are many fine examples of brands that consistently make promises and keep them. These brands:

- Are ranked at the top of *Consumer Reports* magazine product and service ratings (www.consumerreports.org).
- Were awarded the Mobil Five-Star Certification (www.mobiltravelguide.howstuffworks.com).
- Win the American Automobile Association's Five Diamond Awards (www.aaa.com).
- Earn the best satisfaction scores from the American Consumer Satisfaction Index (www.theacsi.org).
- Are recognized for their high reputation ratings by the Harris Interactive Annual Corporate Reputation Survey (www.harrisinteractive.com).
- Support the principles of the Better Business Bureau (www.bbb.org).
- Contribute significantly to philanthropic and nonprofit causes such as Make-A-Wish Foundation of America (www.wish.org).
- Embrace a strategy which results in being among the best organizations to work for (www.greatplacetowork.com/best/list-bestusa).

THOUGHT GUIDE

FIVE WAYS TO KEEP PROMISES

- The companies and organizations that can be trusted are the ones that make a promise and keep it.
- Don't offer customers incentives such as rebates, rain checks, frequent-flyer miles, or points that are difficult or impossible to redeem.

- Make the communication process with customers the best part of their experience, instead of a frustrating one.
- It's important for the executive team of any organization to personally observe the customers' experiences in their most frequent transactions:
  - Call the customer call center once a week at its busiest time and try to purchase a product or service and then try to exchange it or get a refund.
  - If customer service cannot answer calls in three to five minutes, then inform customers how long they can expect to wait.
  - Interact with online customer service weekly and evaluate the experience.
- Consider every message and prompt that is used in voice-mail or e-mail response systems. Are the automated systems easy to use, or are they a delay tactic to avoid responding?
- Decide what kind of experience customers should have, then provide the appropriate level of professional and friendly service to match your promise.
- Here are five rules to avoid broken promises:
  1. Always make customers feel *appreciated* and *cared* about when they have a problem or need help, not just when they make a purchase.
  2. Make your organization's number one goal to have the *happiest customers,* not to be the biggest or fastest growing company around.
  3. When an organization begins to anticipate a merger, acquisition, consolidation, downsizing, or other type of corporate transaction, *focus on keeping customers happy first* and the necessary business details second.
  4. *Measure, recognize, and reward* the associates who actually delight your customers. Focus on how your associates make your customers feel and not whether they just answer the phone or do their daily job.
  5. Develop and commit to a customer *bill of rights.* Make it fundamental to your organization's culture and not just policy.

CHAPTER

Predicting Brand Success

Imagination is more important than knowledge. Knowledge is limited. Imagination encircles the world.

—Albert Einstein

PREDICTING A BRAND'S FUTURE

Having the right promise is the fundamental key to predicting a brand's success. Genuine brands make a promise, and they deliver on that promise consistently, eagerly, and at the customer's convenience. The power of a promise is based first on customer's feelings toward a brand and second on what customers say about a brand to their friends and family.

A promise should appeal to people's "higher" motives. When we talk about higher motives, we are referring to those that inspire people, such as goodness, trust, mercy, happiness, and helping others. In contrast, "lower" motives could be greed, power, arrogance, distrust, and self-absorption.

Understanding the psychic power of a brand requires a different mindset, perspective, and approach from conventional "brand" wisdom. At first glance, you may be thinking that this sounds "out there." However, we are not talking about séances or Ouija boards; we are talking about a disciplined approach to managing a brand's future.

The purpose of this chapter is to explain the importance of being able to predict a brand's future and how to evaluate the

FIGURE 6.1

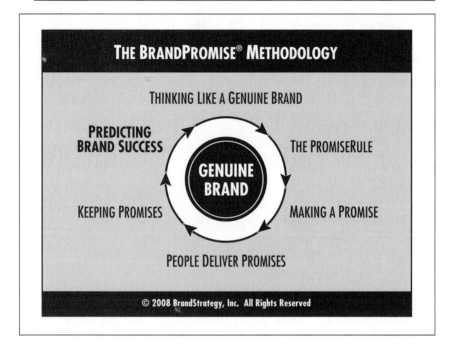

appropriate determinants. As Gerry Grinstein, the former chief executive officer of Delta Airlines explains, "The test of how good you are is out there in the future; it will show whether your strategy was right; it has to stand the test of time."[1]

The BrandPsychic philosophy is based on an understanding that brands have emotional spirits. A brand's emotional spirit resides in the minds and hearts of its associates, customers, consumers, influencers—all of its stakeholders. More often than not, this emotional spirit determines a brand's future success. In order to optimize a brand's future perceptions, an organization must understand the importance of creating positive perceptual brand energy every day.

Our BrandPsychic approach is based on three fundamental concepts:

1. Understanding a brand's perceived spirit or psyche.
2. Visualizing a brand's future.
3. Optimizing positive energy.

FIGURE 6.2

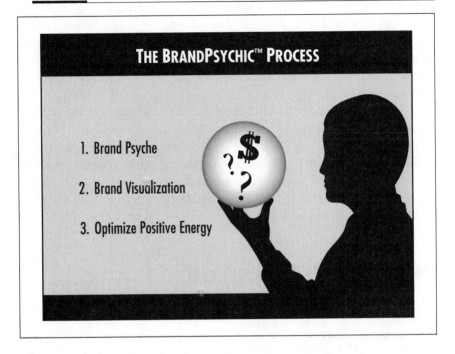

1. BRAND PSYCHE

The first step is to understand a brand's spirit and soul. How a brand is perceived in the hearts and minds of its associates, customers, consumers, and influencers (stakeholders) creates the perceptual map that determines and signals a brand's future.

If one does not understand a brand's current soul, it is impossible to create a successful strategy for the future.

A reliable perceptual map depends on objective research and insightful perspectives based upon on a brand's emotional spirit in the minds of associates, customers, consumers, and influencers as we discussed in Chapter 3.

It is important to measure a brand's perceptual energy in order to create a benchmark for future activities. In order to evaluate a brand's psyche, a comprehensive analysis of a brand's mental balance between emotional attributes and functional reality is also required.

As the CEO of a large retailer said recently, "We spent the last ten years taking the emotion out of our business; it's now time to put it back in." All too often, organizations are so focused on their functional activities that a brand can lose its emotional balance. When brands focus on improving the customers' experience and creating positive energy, great things can happen.

Genuine brands should excel in the functional area of their business and reflect the "best demonstrated practices," such as FedEx, Starbucks, or In-N-Out. However, the key to achieving future success is making sure that a brand is perceived to be delivering distinctive emotional benefits to all its stakeholders. This means that an organization needs to consider how changes in its policies and procedures will make its customers feel.

Measuring a Brand's Perceptual Energy

As we discussed earlier, our intent is to focus on the heart and soul of a brand as one of the determinants of its future success. All too often, customer or market research focuses on questions like, how satisfied are you? Regardless of the answers, this kind of information doesn't provide any insights into how people really feel.

Measuring a brand's perceptual energy begins with how it is perceived today. If it happens to be a major brand, there are all sorts of sources to identify the brand's perceptions. These include *Consumer Reports*, the Harris Interactive, annual corporate reputation surveys, and the University of Michigan's American Customer Satisfaction Index (ACSI.). At any given time, anyone can prepare an analysis of how specific brands or industries are perceived by consumers. The above-mentioned reports and other similar surveys poll thousands of consumers. The results can be combined to create directionally accurate conclusions. If a brand is relatively small and is not included in these surveys, the information they provide may still be very helpful as a guide to understanding the perceptions of a business category or certain competitors. While brand research is generally focused on customers, it is critical to understand how all stakeholders feel as outlined in Figure 6.3.

FIGURE 6.3

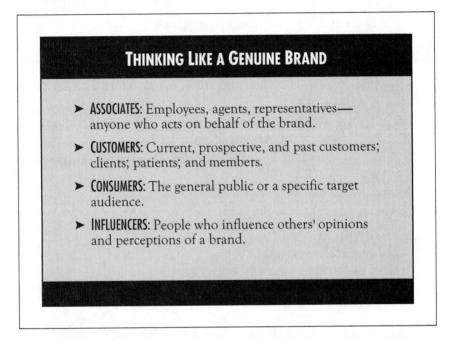

> **THINKING LIKE A GENUINE BRAND**
>
> ➤ **ASSOCIATES:** Employees, agents, representatives—
>   anyone who acts on behalf of the brand.
>
> ➤ **CUSTOMERS:** Current, prospective, and past customers;
>   clients; patients; and members.
>
> ➤ **CONSUMERS:** The general public or a specific target
>   audience.
>
> ➤ **INFLUENCERS:** People who influence others' opinions
>   and perceptions of a brand.

The important thing to note is that these surveys measure and test consumers' perceptions of various brand promises every day. *Consumer Reports* and others are basically providing a free industry perspective for hundreds of brands' perceived promises.

Here's an easy way for any type of organization to quickly and inexpensively get a reality check on its perceptual energy. Whether in person, on the phone, or on the Web, ask questions like the following:

Based on your perception of [insert brand name] today, on a scale from 1 to 10, where 10 is exceptional and 1 is unacceptable, please answer the following questions:

1. How distinctive is our brand in terms of our products and services? _____
2. How relevant is our brand's products and services to your needs? _____

3. How do you perceive our overall value? Please rate our value based on:

The time involved dealing with us _____

The way we make you feel _____

Pricing for our products and services _____

4. Please rate your feelings about your overall experience with our brand. _____

5. Brand trend. Please provide your perceptions of our brand today as compared with two years ago:

	The Same	Declined	Improved
Relevance to your needs	_____	_____	_____
Overall perceived value	_____	_____	_____
Overall brand experience	_____	_____	_____
Our future success	_____	_____	_____

The first set of questions is a basic outline to establish a few fundamental baseline perceptions. These and other selected questions could be asked of 50 random consumers a day or over a week or any other combination of research methodologies. The important thing is to get a weekly reality check on a brand's perceptions currently and where people perceive a brand is going. The questions should be asked of associates, consumers, customers, and influencers on a frequent basis. The old idea of an "annual" survey is passé and not realistically helpful on a timely basis in today's fast-paced marketplace.

An organization can ask these and other questions about a competing brand as well to gain comparative insights. Questions related to which brand does certain things the best or about consumers' "favorite" brands are also great ways to get a 360-degree perspective. While some might consider this approach unscientific, these questions are intended to provide directional information to predict a brand's performance in the future. This information should be triangulated with other regular scientific customer, consumer, and market research to create a comprehensive view of a brand's future.

2. BRAND VISUALIZATION

The second phase of the BrandPsychic methodology involves an understanding of where associates, customers, consumers, and influencers envision a brand to be in the future. Just as in the book *The Secret* by Rhonda Byrne, visualization continually occurs in the stakeholders' minds. This book contains wisdom from modern day teachers who have used it to achieve health, wealth, and happiness.

Visualization is important for two reasons: First, it's critical to know how a brand's stakeholders are visualizing its current position as well as its future. Second, once a brand has decided what it wants to be, it is fundamental to create a situation in which its stakeholders are visualizing a shared perspective for the brand's future.

Believe it or not, your customers, consumers, associates, and influencers are visualizing your brand every day. When a customer tells a friend, "I sure wish they had drive-up or valet services," or an associate says, "I wish my manager was more inspiring," they are visualizing what they would like a brand to be.

If an organization desires to be an exceptional brand, it has to be able to "listen" and appropriately act on these visualizations. Google seems to be able to do this on a daily basis. It's almost like someone says, "I wish I could do that or get this kind of information," and suddenly Google offers it. In order to be in touch with all stakeholders' needs, a brand must have a culture that embraces change and enjoys the "relevancy" challenge. Most brands fail because they become perceived as irrelevant or less relevant based on their customers feelings and needs over time. Yet how many brands ask their customers, on a daily basis, to rate their relevance compared to other brands, and how many ask which brand is the most relevant? It may be a good idea to ask customers which brands they think will be the most relevant to their needs next year.

Hopefully, it's beginning to make sense that unless a brand is listening, understanding, and acting on its customers' visualizations, then it is at risk for a really bad surprise.

Here's the reality. Name a brand that has experienced a major fraud, an earnings disaster, an ousted executive team, severe negative regulatory action, and so on, and you can bet that prior to the problem the brand was already failing in the minds of its customers, consumers, associates, or influencers. In most cases, a brand disaster could have been predicted if someone had listened to the customers' and other stakeholders' visualizations.

Rhonda Byrne says, "When you are visualizing, you are emitting that powerful frequency out into the Universe. The law of attraction will take hold of that powerful signal and return those pictures back to you, just as you saw them in your mind."[2]

Getting everyone involved in the same vision for a genuine brand can become a powerful force. When you come into contact with a genuine brand and everyone is visualizing the same future for it, then you can feel the magnetism and positive energy that seem to emanate throughout the organization.

"Everyone visualizes whether he knows it or not. Visualizing is the great secret of success."[3]

Reading Customers' Minds

An important way to improve a brand's relevance in the minds of customers and associates is to make them feel as though you know what they want. Let's take a typical retail situation. Whether it's a grocery store or discount store, there are certain customer behaviors that are predictable as outlined in Figure 6.4. If a customer is in an aisle looking perplexed at two or three products, she probably has a question that an associate could answer and help her make the choice. Unfulfilled, this doubt may lead to indecision and a lost sale.

Associates can be trained to spot these behaviors and approach the customer, not with the, "Hi, how are you?" but with, "May I be of assistance?" If the associate doesn't know the answer, then he or she should be able to find a manager who does. If a customer is hurriedly going through the aisles looking all around, he is probably looking for something he can't find. Hence, associates who have been trained to recognize the five basic retail customer predictors, can often make customers feel as if the associates know what they want. Everyone has a shortage of time and is willing to invest only a limited amount of

FIGURE 6.4

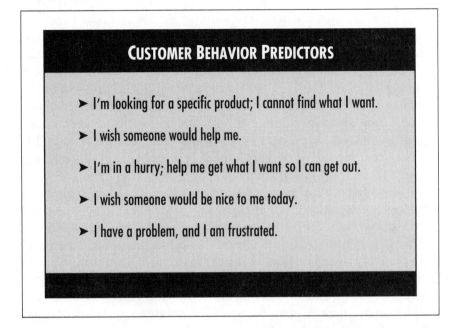

CUSTOMER BEHAVIOR PREDICTORS

➤ I'm looking for a specific product; I cannot find what I want.

➤ I wish someone would help me.

➤ I'm in a hurry; help me get what I want so I can get out.

➤ I wish someone would be nice to me today.

➤ I have a problem, and I am frustrated.

effort in the retail or online routine. The secret is to visualize what customers need to improve a brand's success.

Another way to predict a brand's future is to examine perceptions outside the target market. For instance, if a brand represents a baby-boomer luxury product, find out how young professionals feel about it. They are the next crop of customers. If a brand has teenage target market, find out how parents perceive the brand. If a brand is related to outdoor winter sports, find out what travelers think who don't ski or snowboard. Insights from other consumers can help with messaging and visualization in order to create positive brand influencers outside the target market. People who do not drink coffee understand the attraction of Starbucks. Predicting a brand's future success requires a nontraditional mindset and an open-mindedness to a holistic approach to perceptions.

We've discussed Brand Balance extensively in previous chapters; however, it's worth expanding in relation to predicting a brand's future. The first rule is that if a brand is not perceived distinctively on an emotional basis, it will not become a genuine brand.

"Many product-centric companies probably start out with a focus on customers. But after early successes, they institutionalize the notion that markets respond primarily to great products and services," according to Ranjay Gulati in the *Harvard Business Review*.[4]

This product preoccupation is also linked to the lack of a promise, because many organizations act like the product is the promise. When competitors provide similar products, the brand's lack of an emotional differentiation confirms customers' perceptions that there isn't really a meaningful difference. This leads to a commodity perception. True loyalty does not develop merely from frequent purchases; the balance of positive emotional and functional perceptions is needed in order to create a long-term competitive advantage.

Hence, customer and market research focused solely on product attributes will not provide a sound basis for predicting a brand's future success. Asking customers, consumers, and influencers questions about how they feel about a brand specifically and compared to other brands can help, but until a brand understands how its customers, associates, and influencers *want* to feel, it's difficult to look into the future.

Convenience Is the Future

When consumers decide to pay some of their bills by direct checking, they call a mortgage, cable, auto loan company, or whatever. It may be a surprise to learn that most of these businesses send a form by mail; the consumers must complete the form and send it back. It usually takes a month or two for a regular automatic withdrawal to be processed. Why would any company make it inconvenient to get its customers' money immediately?

If you want to pay your American Express bill by direct withdrawal, you simply call the company, and it's done. No delay, no forms to complete. American Express even knows if you have enough money in your checking account to pay the bill.

Every organization has the challenge of constantly innovating to enhance its brand in the future and to maintain or gain a competitive advantage. All too often, companies' innovation attempts turn out to be a waste of time or failures. The

FIGURE 6.5

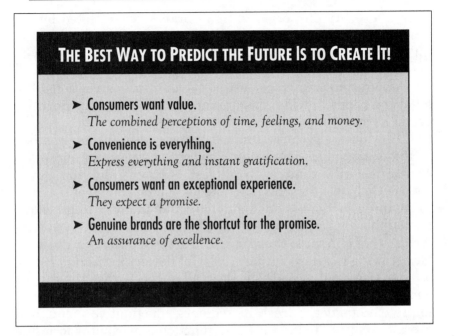

THE BEST WAY TO PREDICT THE FUTURE IS TO CREATE IT!

➤ Consumers want value.
The combined perceptions of time, feelings, and money.

➤ Convenience is everything.
Express everything and instant gratification.

➤ Consumers want an exceptional experience.
They expect a promise.

➤ Genuine brands are the shortcut for the promise.
An assurance of excellence.

secret to brand innovations that really make a difference and enhance a brand's future success is to change the playing field or business model so that it makes it difficult for competitors to keep up. This type of innovation is discussed in Chapter 4 as a paradigm shift.

Let's look at some paradigm shift examples:

- *3M Post-it brand notes:*   Suddenly anything that stuck permanently was history.
- *Drive-up windows:*   If you're trying to sell fast food or coffee and you don't have a drive-up window, forget it.
- *Ziploc Storage Bags:*   It's hard to imagine storing food any other way.

What is your brand's convenience strategy? Is it overnight or next month? If you're not selling convenience, don't bother selling. Who would buy a flat-screen television, at any price, without a remote?

3. OPTIMIZE POSITIVE ENERGY

Each and every day, organization's brands are affected by the positive and negative feelings of their customers, associates, and influencers. It's important that every brand have a strategy to optimize the positive feelings and minimize the negative feelings in order to create the best possible future perceptions. The following pages provide insights into how to minimize negative brand karma.

How does a great restaurant make and fulfill its promise? In the Napa Valley, chef Cindy Pawlcyn's famous restaurants—Mustards Grill, Cindy's Backstreet Kitchen, and the newly opened Go Fish—demonstrate a keen understanding of the need to balance functional and emotional value in order to provide a memorable experience for guests. External details such as architecture that enhances the experience of the food, organic vegetables growing in raised gardens, colorful flowers in window boxes, or fruit trees just outside the door, all suggest what the experience inside will be from a functional viewpoint: stylish yet unpretentious decor, fresh ingredients, imaginative menu, and overall attention to detail. These functional attributes form the basis of a dining experience that is much more than the sum of the parts. Pawlcyn calls it, "Good food for good value," and that standard extends to the whole experience, from parking lot to plate to the welcoming atmosphere that makes each customer feel like a guest.

How people feel is the ultimate and most important part of the experience, and Pawlcyn's underlying promise is that everyone who enters will feel comfortable and special. People coming from a memorial service, a wedding, or a hike in the hills all blend happily in the environment she creates. "We're trying to create an environment," she said recently, "where everyone, whether dressed up or in casual attire, is having the same great experience." That experience does not happen by accident; she and her staff work at it, meeting and training every day to be able to create not just great food and great service, but a genuine connection with customers.

This genuine connection can make the difference between success and a customer who never returns. Pawlcyn tells her staff that if they show that they really care about their customers, when something goes wrong, the customers will give them a chance to fix it. If they don't make that connection and something goes wrong, the customer will leave with a bad impression—and tell others. A recent customer was hoping to enjoy Pawlcyn's signature coffee crème brûlée, and found to her dismay it had disappeared from the menu. Though the restaurant was very busy, the waiter listened with compassion to the customer's wail of disappointment and then explained with care why the menu had changed. He described the new choices with such charm that the customer was won over. When the new dessert arrived, all was more than forgiven. The guest may not have gotten the crème brûlée, but she did get the happy dessert experience she expected when coming to Cindy's.

A genuine promise, which is functional and emotional and which holds up in times when things go awry, creates a loyal following. For Pawlcyn, it's no secret: "Be consistent, always use the best, and keep it simple."

Spending Time on the Right Things

Another way to measure the positive energy that a brand creates is to ask an organization's associates, managers, and executives how they spend their time. An anonymous survey of a reasonable sample of a brand's representatives related to how they spend their time can be very insightful. Survey questions could include:

What percentage of your day is involved in:

- Handling day-to-day operational responsibilities?
- Motivating and inspiring other associates?
- Delighting customers?
- Solving problems that another associate did not take care of?

The kinds of insights provided by the answers to these questions can help organizations decide what it wants its executives, managers, and frontline associates to focus on. Our research indicates that leaders of organizations have a significant opportunity to enhance positive emotional energy. The more the focus is on the daily functional "to dos," the less emotional energy is available to enhance the brand's future success.

Setting the right example for associates starts at the top. If you call the corporate offices of Hickory Farms and ask the receptionist to connect you to the chief executive officer, she doesn't screen your call; she connects you with his office. Even more surprising, there's a good chance John "J" Langdon will actually answer the phone; it happened to me twice! John believes in the philosophy that, "The customer is the boss and that everyone's job at Hickory Farms is to help customers, whenever possible." By setting this example, all levels of executives and associates at Hickory Farms have a service orientation and understand that the customer is the reason the brand succeeds.

It may be that "Midwest effect," which is a certain kind of sincerity and "down-to-earth" philosophy that distinguishes brands like Hickory Farms and makes you want to do business with them. There is even a Farmer's Handshake Guarantee. One thing is for sure—a brand's future success requires that everyone practice the right behavior today.

INVESTING IN A BRAND'S FUTURE

As we have illustrated, the key to a genuine brand's success is connecting with all its stakeholders on an emotional level. One way to accomplish a long-term emotional connection is for organizations to be socially conscious of consumers' and associates' higher values as they relate to other people, the environment, or whatever. This strategy can also provide a positive emotional reserve when challenges occur.

This new reality is referred to as *corporate social responsibility* (CSR). Some organizations might look at this as doing the right thing, while others may be more interested in the profit opportunity. CSR should be viewed as an investment in a brand's emotional future. When it's done right, CSR can be a win for everyone. As an example, going "green" or building a "green" facility may create positive emotional dividends for years to come.

"All of a sudden, corporate responsibility is an idea whose time has arrived," says Julie Fox Gorte, chief social investment strategist at the Calvert Group, which manages socially responsible mutual funds. "We're seeing more companies who think it's not just a philosophy, but good for business too."[5]

More important than just the short-term benefits is the opportunity to achieve a positive long-term visualization benefit for a brand. Organizations that implement an appropriate CSR strategy can positively affect future growth, profits, stakeholder loyalty, and real competitive advantage. As an example, Toyota's hybrid strategy has created an enormous financial and competitive advantage as well as enhancing the Toyota brand's spirit in the hearts and souls of consumers worldwide.

A review of 52 studies of 34,000 organizations by the University of Redlands' Marc Orlitsky and the University of Iowa's Sara Rynes and Frank Schmidt concluded, "that well-run, profitable businesses also boasted strong social and environmental records, and vice versa. Overwhelmingly, firms that rewarded employees with good work climates and higher pay and benefits ultimately saw stronger sales and stock prices, plus less employee turnover."[6]

MINIMIZE NEGATIVE ENERGY

Every dissatisfied or disappointed customer has the potential to sabotage the perception of a brand's future and ultimately its success. In order to be able to predict a brand's future, it is enormously important to minimize negative perceptions and the risk to a brand's future as a result of negative experiences.

It's interesting to note that problem resolution is often the number one issue for financial institution customers. Many customers also indicated they had switched brands because of the lack of appropriate problem resolution. If any kind of problem resolution, such as refunds, credits or other issues, is the most frequent source of frustration for customers, then the brand should fix the policies or establish a customer Bill of Rights as we discussed in Chapter 5. The strategy should be to eliminate as much negative energy related to customer dissatisfaction as possible.

When executives discuss customer service problems, they are generally referring to them in the past or present tense. But unsatisfying customer experiences and negative associate attitudes affect a brand's future prospects. The situation may happen today, but the results will influence the brand's success tomorrow.

As long as customers are not thieves, why would any organization make its customers unhappy? Is it really worth the negative perceptual energy to make a customer unhappy? Everyone knows that customers tell many more people about their unhappy experiences than their satisfying ones. Therefore, if a brand wants to optimize its positive energy, it needs many more wonderful customer experiences to make up for a few bad ones.

The opportunity to learn and improve as a result of dissatisfied customers is a huge opportunity. As Bill Gates says, "Your most unhappy customers are your greatest source of learning."[7]

The traditional approach today related to customer service problems seems to be focused on a brand's associates explaining the "policy." Then the fun begins, and the associate and consumer argue over the policy when they should be discussing a mutually acceptable solution. Regardless of the outcome, this approach usually creates lots of negative feelings for everyone involved.

Enlightened brands are following a different approach in order to eliminate negative energy related to customer service problems. They are discovering the value of an approach that is focused on an understanding first and a solution second with the ultimate goal of a happy customer. This protocol is as follows:

1. Listen and understand how the customer feels.
2. Acknowledge the customers' feelings and identify with their emotions in a dialogue that makes them feel appreciated.
3. Ask the customer, what can I do to make you happy today?
4. Agree upon a solution or investigate a solution and get back to the customer ASAP.

Most unhappy customers want to feel appreciated and understood. Yet our research indicates that sincere apologies and compassion are in short supply. Surprisingly, when customers are asked what will make them happy, their requests are usually reasonable. Responding appropriately to their requests makes them feel empowered. Regardless of the ultimate solution, if customers don't feel good, the result is negative brand energy.

Leading executives refer to this enlightened approach as a positive "recovery strategy." A *recovery strategy* focuses on maintaining customer goodwill based on the belief that a customer's financial and emotional contributions to a brand's equity over time is fundamentally important. The recovery concept is based on the reality that, regardless of the business or enterprise, problems are a normal part of everyday existence. The distinction of a recovery mindset is that every problem, especially typical customer dissatisfaction, presents an opportunity to actually enhance customer loyalty.

Here's an example of the basis for a recovery strategy. Research clearly indicates that in a typical business there is a measurable rate of satisfaction when customers are happy. The fact is that when a generally satisfied customer has a problem and the brand addresses that problem in a favorable manner, that customer's satisfaction actually can be higher than when things are normally okay.

For organizations, there is a real incentive to employ a recovery strategy that turns dissatisfied customers into brand advocates for the following reasons:

1. Every customer represents an opportunity to create future financial and emotional brand equity.
2. Each dialogue with a customer is an opportunity to enhance brand loyalty.
3. Customers' perceptions after a successful problem resolution can actually increase satisfaction levels.
4. Positive brand energy enhances a brand's future equity.

Most importantly, a recovery strategy minimizes negative energy as well as future brand risk while enhancing the prospects for success.

Typically there is a lot of negative brand energy that's created around returning merchandise. The typical disappointments include:

- Returning a product and being frustrated by a delayed credit.

- Receiving a product that doesn't fit or is not what was expected.
- Returning a product requires a call to a different customer service number. It's not usually toll free, they don't answer, there is a wait for an authorization (or, a "call tag"), and the customer has to pay to ship the product back.

Zappos.com understands the negative energy concept and has created an experience that optimizes positive perceptions instead of negative ones:

- Zappos focuses on fast delivery as a brand experience.
- Every product that is ordered is available for shipment.
- Returning a purchase is easy. Customers can go online 24/7 for the authorization, and it is provided immediately with a paid return shipping label.
- Convenient help is always available with a call to the company's 24/7 customer call center.

Their company philosophy is a great example; it believes that customer service isn't just a function but that it is really the entire company. As an example, every new employee who is hired for the corporate office "is required to go through 4 weeks of customer loyalty training (answering phones in [their] call center)."[8]

Zappos delivers on its promise; "Powered by Service." It's clear that it has really thought about how to minimize negative brand equity and employed this strategy to create a paradigm shift. It has been rewarded with amazing success. Since its founding in 1999, sales have increased to more than a half a billion dollars annually.

The secret to predicting a brand's success is for an organization to consistently focus on enhancing it's relevance in prospective and current customers' minds.

THOUGHT GUIDE

PREDICTING BRAND SUCCESS

- A promise should appeal to customers' higher motives, such as trust, goodness, happiness, and mercy.

- Every brand has an emotional spirit; understanding that spirit can unlock a brand's full potential.
- How customers, associates, consumers, and influencers visualize a brand's future provides an important perspective.
- In order to enjoy long-term success, a brand's culture must embrace change and use it to its advantage. The best way to predict change is to create it.
- Associates' ability to read customers' wants and needs creates an environment that builds positive relationships between associates and customers and promotes mutual confidence.
- Customer's most frequent desires are predictable. Here are a few:
  1. I'm looking for a specific product; I cannot find what I want.
  2. I wish someone would help me.
  3. I'm in a hurry; help me get what I want so I can get out.
  4. I wish someone would be nice to me today.
  5. I have a problem, and I am frustrated.
- How executives, management, and associates spend their time directly affects customers' experiences and their brand perceptions.
- The distinction of a recovery mindset is that every problem, especially typical customer dissatisfaction, presents an opportunity to actually enhance customer loyalty.
- For organizations, there is a real incentive to employ a recovery strategy that turns dissatisfied customers into brand advocates for the following reasons:
  1. Every customer represents an opportunity to create future financial and emotional brand equity.
  2. Each dialogue with a customer is an opportunity to enhance brand loyalty.
  3. Customers' perceptions after a successful problem resolution can actually increase satisfaction levels.
  4. Positive brand energy enhances a brand's future equity.

CHAPTER 7

Community Brands: The Destination BrandPromise

The true worth of your travels lies not in where you come to be at journey's end, but in the lives you touch along the way.

—Author Unknown

DETAILED EXAMPLE OF THE BRANDPROMISE METHODOLOGY

This chapter provides a detailed outline of how to apply the BrandPromise methodology to communities and destinations. We thought it would be more interesting to apply the methodology to a different type of situation as opposed to the traditional corporate or product brand initiative. While the methodology is generally the same for all types of applications, the following pages outline the right way to create genuine brand experiences and real promises for communities.

COMMUNITY BRANDS

Communities are working together like never before to promote their common brand. It is not uncommon today for a community-wide brand initiative to include chambers of commerce, economic development agencies, destination marketing organizations, city

141

141

and county governments, airports, convention centers, and other civic representatives.

While various community agencies may have somewhat different missions, they all have the same interest in creating an exceptional "destination" that is attractive to residents, businesses, visitors, new investment, and development. As Jack Moneypenny, former vice president of Visit Milwaukee explains, "The bottom line is that partnerships work. It's not just true in our industry, partnerships are proving to be very effective elsewhere, but it's just that the destination marketing industry turns out to be particularly conducive to partnerships."[1]

The BrandPromise methodology has been widely utilized by every kind of community organization to create successful strategies. This chapter will focus on applying the BrandPromise methodology to a community brand from the perspective of a travel and tourism destination.

As Gary Lawrence, CEO of the Lubbock (Texas) Economic Development Alliance, says, "Tourism is the purest form of economic development."

Communities understand the importance that a brand is not just a logo or an advertising campaign; it is all about the value of making a promise. New York City mayor Mike Bloomberg is obsessed with taking care of his residents and visitors, that is, customers: establishing 24-hour call lines, collecting data to help develop new products, and sending his executives into the field to solicit feedback directly from the community. "Good companies listen to their customers, No. 1," he says. "Then they try to satisfy their needs, No. 2."[2]

The BrandScience for destinations that is detailed in this chapter focuses on the visitor, or guest, perspective. However, it can be applied to any community organization that truly wants to make and keep a promise. Communities around the world have used these principles to enhance their brand success.

DESTINATION STRATEGY

When was the last time you were on vacation or a business trip and experienced a specific destination that was remarkable and unforgettable? Think about how you felt about your trip. What made this experience distinctive?

As the tourism marketplace becomes more competitive, it is essential that destinations continue to define themselves. Every destination has positive attributes, but these alone may not be enough to attract guests because there are other similar destinations vying for the same guests. Destinations must work to define themselves in a manner that truly offers guests a remarkable experience so that guests and tourism revenues do not go elsewhere, or they risk losing the competitive edge.

Guests have myriad choices when determining where to travel, and each destination must ensure that it is perceived as unique and distinctive. What gives a destination a competitive edge over similarly perceived destinations or other choices? The answer is the "Destination Promise," the strategic mindset that makes a destination unique in the minds of guests, influencers, and stakeholders.

We use the term *guests* because destinations have a responsibility to view visitors as guests. The word *guest* denotes someone who's been invited and therefore has expectations. It also means that there is a strong emotional connection to being entertained and receiving other things that guests might expect from a host.

From a destination organization's perspective, *influencers* refer to professionals involved with setting up and arranging meetings, conventions, conferences, and travel-related media, and businesses that "influence" and direct guests to destinations for business or pleasure, or both.

Stakeholders refer to a destination's or community's organization's members (members of a convention and visitors bureau, such as a chamber of commerce or economic development agency), tourism businesses, government agencies, residents, and others who may be viewed as "hosts."

A destination's strategy should answer the following questions:

- What should our destination's distinctive promise be?
- What does our destination stand for in the minds of the key stakeholders?
- What BrandPromise experience should be communicated by our tourism representatives to our current and potential guests, influencers, and other stakeholders?

- Are we dedicated to providing an exceptional experience for every guest?
- What is the consensus regarding the optimum brand image and future position for our destination?
- What is the most effective way to use marketing and other promotional aids to gain competitive advantage and increase our destination's success?
- What is the first word that we want to come to mind when prospective guests and influencers think of our destination?
- What brand attributes are important to our destination's varied stakeholders?

Consider this, more than five decades ago Walt Disney had an inspiration to not only open an amusement park but to create an overall experience that would make "dreams come true." When you enter one of Disney's resort parks, it is like entering a magical world where memories will be created and where you will have a unique experience. How did Disney imagine such an idea? His focus was always on creating the experience for guests first and product second: "The Happiest Place on Earth." The company is dedicated to its promise that: "Cast members turn the ordinary into the extraordinary."

DESTINATION BRANDSCIENCE

Our proprietary methodology for building genuine destination brands was articulated in the book *Destination BrandScience*, published by the Destination Marketing Association International. This guide outlines the disciplined process by which a destination organization can make a unique and meaningful contribution to the economic viability of a community beyond routine travel and tourism promotions.

FIGURE 7.1

THINK LIKE A BRAND

"To be a brand, one doesn't just say, I am a brand, therefore I am. It is close, but not quite. To be a brand, one has to first THINK LIKE A BRAND. Thinking like a brand requires a different mindset, perspective and approach from business as usual."

—Michael Gehrisch, President, Destination Marketing Association International

Used with permission.

In short, it is this promise of creating a unique destination experience that becomes the cornerstone of all strategic planning, actions, and future decision making for a successful destination brand.

The Destination BrandScience process is outlined in Figure 7.2. The process consists of five phases of a comprehensive and strategic analysis of a destination.

1. *Brand Assessment:* This is the research phase in which a destination conducts surveys of guests, community stakeholders, leaders, local businesses, residents, city staff, and city officials to determine perspectives

related to the current strengths, weaknesses, and attributes of the destination.

2. *BrandPromise:* In this phase, the research, perceptions, and opportunities are analyzed, and the results determine what core benefits and visitor experiences will make a destination a compelling one.

3. *Brand Blueprint:* Building on the promise as a foundation, a destination develops the communication strategy to optimize its visual and emotional perceptions to become distinctive in the guests' minds.

4. *Brand Culturalization:* The community lives and breathes the brand and provides the right experience. A destination's message will be conveyed in printed training materials, communications, and all customer relations throughout the destination.

FIGURE 7.2

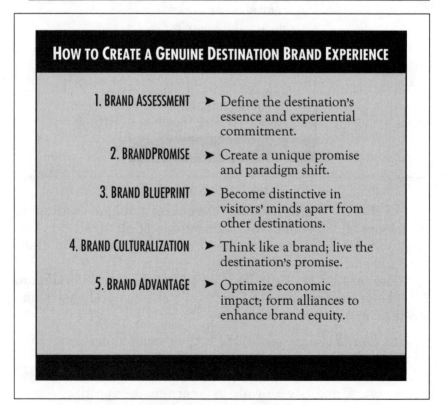

HOW TO CREATE A GENUINE DESTINATION BRAND EXPERIENCE

1. BRAND ASSESSMENT ➤ Define the destination's essence and experiential commitment.

2. BRANDPROMISE ➤ Create a unique promise and paradigm shift.

3. BRAND BLUEPRINT ➤ Become distinctive in visitors' minds apart from other destinations.

4. BRAND CULTURALIZATION ➤ Think like a brand; live the destination's promise.

5. BRAND ADVANTAGE ➤ Optimize economic impact; form alliances to enhance brand equity.

5. *Brand Advantage:* Community partnership in a destination optimizes its economic impact and creates alliances to enhance brand equity.

PROMISING AN EXPERIENCE

Community leaders should follow a strategy that results in their destination being perceived as distinctive from other choices, being more relevant to their guests and influencers, and offering superior perceived value.

In today's challenging environment, convention and visitors bureaus, tourism boards, and destination marketing organizations are expected to provide brand leadership for their members, not just promote a destination. A successful destination must think like a genuine brand from two perspectives (as a destination and as a convention and visitors bureau or destination marketing organization), and this requires a mindset, perspective, and strategy that is different from business as usual. Successful destinations need to be perceived as distinctive and need to make a promise to their guests that delivers emotional and functional benefits. The Destination Marketing Association International created a directional promise for its member organizations that is shown in Figure 7.3. Chapter 9 includes a detailed examination of the Destination Marketing Association International's Brand Leadership Project.

Convention and visitors bureaus and tourism boards are perfectly positioned to be brand stewards for destinations. Destinations can distinguish themselves, develop a promise, increase revenues and profits, and create a better environment for the guest, which results in a unique destination experience that becomes the cornerstone for all strategic planning, actions, and future decision making.

When a destination thinks and acts like a genuine brand, the entire community understands what the promise is and how it can deliver the right experience, as illustrated in Figure 7.4. Leading destination organizations that deliver on their promise to their members and guests will benefit from enhanced member satisfaction and visitor demand that provide profitable pricing opportunities for the business community, an increase in pride and tax benefits, as well as the power of a positive

FIGURE 7.3

experience. The key for a destination to become a successful genuine brand is to focus on providing distinctive and relevant experiences that enrich the guest and provide lasting and memorable impressions.

A great brand is more than just name recognition. It is an emotional attachment to the product and an expectation of service or quality that consistently leaves the consumer feeling delighted regardless of the price paid. Genuine brands are cultivated and developed, not organically grown. In the case of destinations, in order for them to compete, they must be more than simply a place to visit. They must produce an emotional connection with the consumer that transcends just products and services, such as attractions or things to do, or price points.

FIGURE 7.4

A WELL-WRITTEN PROMISE

"A well-written promise gives potential visitors a mental picture of themselves enjoying your destination. The proper depiction conveyed in the promise will offer an overall feeling and a realistic expectation of what experiences awaits them."

—Rob Stern
Destination Marketing
Association International

Used with permission.

There is nothing like visiting a destination that provides a unique, exceptional experience.

Thinking like a brand requires a different mindset, and the promise is the key to this unique approach. It is absolutely fundamental to creating, developing, or enhancing a new or existing genuine destination brand.

WHAT IS A DESTINATION BRANDPROMISE?

A destination should be about a promise. A destination's promise to guests needs to deliver on the core attributes that a destination "owns" and on key attributes that it desires to own. This commitment will lead a destination to the ultimate goal of becoming a one-of-a-kind destination and genuine brand.

A promise *communicates* three inherent attributes:

- Something will be *done.*
- There is an expressed emotional *assurance.*
- There is a perception of *future excellence* and achievement.

A promise should be written to define the intended functional and emotional benefits from the guest's point of view after experiencing a destination's products and services. Because it incorporates the guest's viewpoint, a promise is distinctly different from a mission or vision statement. The promise represents a destination's commitment to its guests, members, and influencers and how it wants them to feel. It reflects the essence (*heart, soul,* and *spirit*) of the benefits (*functional* and *emotional*) that guests, influencers, and stakeholders should expect to receive when experiencing a brand's products and services.

Creating a strategy for a destination requires a discipline that is focused on a promise that will be offered in order to create a distinctive and valued perception that results in "preference" or "insistence" that is much more desirable than other competing destinations. Travel and tourism destinations must continually examine themselves and their image to occupy a relevant position in their guests' and influencers' minds.

The promise should serve as the guiding star for everything a destination does. The primary purpose of the promise is to communicate clearly what the destination stands for to every guest, member, employee, agent, representative, and so on, associated with a destination. This is illustrated in Figure 7.5, Santa Monica's promise.

Destination brands must focus on answering three primary questions in order to develop an effective promise:

- What kind of experience should our destination be about?
- What distinguishes our products and services from competitors?
- What is superior about the value we offer our stakeholders?

FIGURE 7.5

Santa Monica…the best way to discover L.A.; an unforgettable beach city experience filled with eye-catching people, cutting-edge culture and bold innovations. **It is the essence of the California lifestyle.**

Used with permission.

Guests develop their perception of value through a subjective *feeling* as a result of comparing what a destination has to offer with what its competitors are offering based on their own needs, preferences, buying behavior, and personal characteristics. Thus, *perceptions* of value constantly change. Consequently, the ability to deliver value and *delight* stakeholders is deeply rooted in the promise. Growth comes from serving guests and members *better* and concentrating on a destination's *distinctive competence.*

DESTINATION BRAND ASSESSMENT

Tourism is the lifeblood of many communities and allows a destination's residents to enjoy many benefits that otherwise would not be part of their lifestyle. However, communities are constantly being challenged to attract guests. The question remains, what will give one destination a competitive edge over similarly perceived destinations or other choices? The answer is a *Destination Brand*, the strategic asset that makes destinations unique in the minds of their guests, influencers, and stakeholders.

If any resident was asked to describe a city to a potential visitor, what would he or she say? Many cities can lay claim to the same attributes. Therefore, how can a destination be distinctive compared to other destinations and compete in the leisure, meetings, conventions, and independent guest market?

We recommend that a Brand Assessment be a consultative process that involves guests, influencers, board, staff, members, and key stakeholders to help evaluate the relevancy of a destination's current brand positioning and to move forward with understanding, retaining, refining, or reinventing a promise as outlined in Figure 7.6.

The ultimate objectives of the process are threefold. The first objective is to discover how guests, influencers, and stakeholders currently perceive a destination. The second objective is to determine how a destination wants guests, influencers, and stakeholders to answer the question: What is our destination's promise? The third objective is to determine how a destination's tourism industry and the community at large would guide the delivery of a "promised experience."

A destination should desire to optimize the clarity and legibility of its current visual image, refresh the look and feel of its current identity, and establish brand guidelines for all media activities. Guest and stakeholder destination brand research serves as a diagnostic tool to clarify exactly where a destination is now and what can be done to improve or enhance its position in the future. The data that are collected are crucial to the success of a destination brand development process.

This fundamental philosophy will guide sales, marketing, and servicing efforts. The promise reflects the essence (heart, soul, and spirit) of the benefits (functional and emotional) that guests, influencers, and stakeholders receive when experiencing a brand's products and services.

A destination's strategy for its brand is the critical driver that will guide the direction of the positioning and perception of a destination and its associated brand values.

FIGURE 7.6

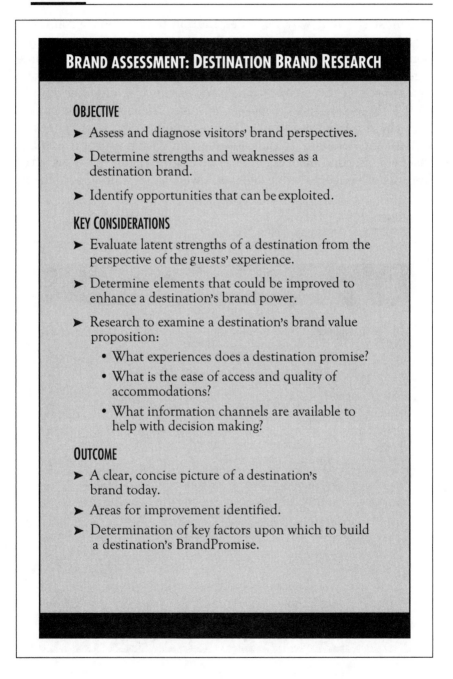

BRAND ASSESSMENT: DESTINATION BRAND RESEARCH

OBJECTIVE

➤ Assess and diagnose visitors' brand perspectives.

➤ Determine strengths and weaknesses as a destination brand.

➤ Identify opportunities that can be exploited.

KEY CONSIDERATIONS

➤ Evaluate latent strengths of a destination from the perspective of the guests' experience.

➤ Determine elements that could be improved to enhance a destination's brand power.

➤ Research to examine a destination's brand value proposition:

- What experiences does a destination promise?
- What is the ease of access and quality of accommodations?
- What information channels are available to help with decision making?

OUTCOME

➤ A clear, concise picture of a destination's brand today.

➤ Areas for improvement identified.

➤ Determination of key factors upon which to build a destination's BrandPromise.

CREATING A DESTINATION BRANDPROMISE

The most efficient way for a destination to develop a promise is for a brand committee, which is usually composed of key destination executives and knowledgeable community leaders, to come together to first review the key conclusions from an objective assessment of the destination. Each committee member should craft a three-sentence proposed promise. These should be copied onto the flip chart and left in a visible place for participants to look at and consider. If complete agreement on a promise is not reached, a second meeting should be called within the week after the initial concepts have been allowed to sit and marinate in

FIGURE 7.7

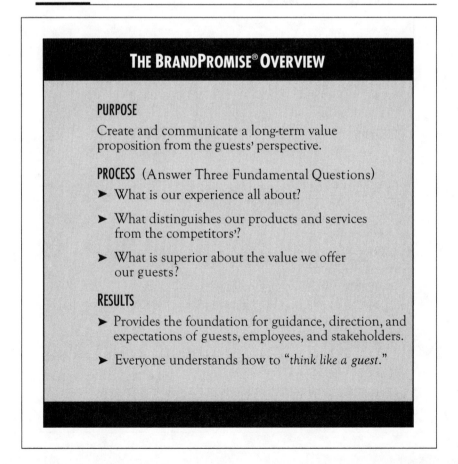

THE BRANDPROMISE® OVERVIEW

PURPOSE

Create and communicate a long-term value proposition from the guests' perspective.

PROCESS (Answer Three Fundamental Questions)

➤ What is our experience all about?

➤ What distinguishes our products and services from the competitors'?

➤ What is superior about the value we offer our guests?

RESULTS

➤ Provides the foundation for guidance, direction, and expectations of guests, employees, and stakeholders.

➤ Everyone understands how to "*think like a guest.*"

people's minds. At the second meeting, the group should establish some consensus on the key elements of the promise even though the exact wording may not be clear. It is important that this process, while critical, should not be drawn out or turned into a lengthy discussion. A drawn-out discussion often overthinks the issues and muddles the outcome. The entire process should include reasonable community updates until there is consensus. The process is outlined in Figure 7.7.

Ultimately, the promise should reflect a balance between the aspirations of a destination brand as well as the reality of what a destination brand can and is capable of delivering to its guests. It's important to note that a promise should be aspirational enough to reach for the stars with the understanding that successful

FIGURE 7.8

THE PROMISE

"The BrandPromise tells the community and future customers that the destination is committed to an outstanding experience level and assures their trust is well placed."

—Michael Gehrisch, President, Destination Marketing Association International

Used with permission.

destination promises reflect a constant migratory journey to fulfill commitments.

After a brand committee has agreed on the right BrandPromise, it is wise to quietly evaluate it with guests and key stakeholders as well as influential community leaders, utilizing our proprietary survey. Greater consensus on the wording and nature of promise will ensure its acceptance and buy-in by the community at large.

A destination's promise comes to life when it is understood by each and every one associated with the destination and when the promise is delivered with flawless execution and the highest level of performance. When the guests benefit from the delivery of a destination's promise, the brand is real.

Genuine brands make a promise, and they deliver that promise consistently, enthusiastically, and at the guests' convenience. A genuine brand creates relationships with guests centered on its promise. The power of a promise is based on what guests say about a destination brand to their friends and about their feelings toward the brand. Word of mouth can be one of the most important determinants of a brand's ultimate success.

A SLOGAN IS NOT A STRATEGY

A genuine destination brand is not simply the result of a catchy slogan or advertising message. It seems as though every couple of days, some destination is announcing its new slogan. The following headlines tell the story:

"Need a Fast Buck? Come Up with a Slogan"
"Baltimore Launches New Tagline"
"New Seattle Tourism Tagline Unveiled"
"St. Louis' Stylish New Tagline"

Unfortunately, it seems that slogans come and go all too often. Millions of dollars are wasted on slogans and advertising taglines that don't work. Of course, it's easy to second-guess any advertising slogan or campaign.

Situations like this illuminate several important issues. For example, no leading computer manufacturer would knowingly put the Intel logo on a computer without the Intel chip actually being inside. "Intel Inside" delivers a promise of performance and hopefully an exceptional experience for the consumer.

Destinations should be the same. Long before anyone even thinks about a slogan, a destination should create a comprehensive strategy that includes a promise. A destination's promise must be linked to an experience that has been well-thought-out and one that is focused on how a destination wants its guests to feel.

A destination and its entire community including government, residents, and visitor industry employees (taxi drivers, public safety, police, fire, restaurant, hotel and convention center) must put a plan in motion to deliver that desired promise and experience. Everyone involved in the visitor's experience is responsible for how a destination's guests feel and their perceptions. This is not to say that a well-conceived slogan cannot contribute to a destination's success. However, a slogan or advertising theme should be based on the desired promise.

Las Vegas is a good example with its most memorable advertising slogan being, "What happens here, stays here." Las Vegas's promise is all about having fun. Hence, Las Vegas's promise is reinforced by the tagline. As a further testament to the importance of the "right" promise, Las Vegas tried for years to promote itself as a family destination. Obviously, it didn't work; it was an emotional disconnect with the destination's promise and its guests' perceptions.

Las Vegas's success as a destination is further enhanced by its airport. The Las Vegas area is growing dramatically, serving almost 50 million people a year. Yet travelers rated it number one according to a 2006 J.D. Power survey.[3] What could be a more important part of the promise?—a destination's airport and its perceptions in the minds of guests.

At the end of the day, a destination is only that which is perceived in the customers' and consumers' minds, or what is called the "mind's eye." A genuine brand adds value to people's lives. It's about benefiting the guests and those who influence guests. Destination brands must be distinctive, and they have to deliver a promise that provides functional and emotional benefits to the guests. According to Marcy Jarret, executive director of Visit Lubbock, "In order to be relevant as a Destination Marketing Organization in the future, we need to be more than

FIGURE 7.9

SOURCE: Getty Images — Photographer, Tom Brakefield; used with permission.

the cheerleaders who deliver balloons to an event. We need to become economic developers."

A destination should develop a unique position in the target customer's mind's eye, based on an emotional attachment. The more distinctive a destination's functional and emotional benefits become in the guests' and influencers' minds, the closer it approaches the definition of a genuine brand. Knowing this, a destination can differentiate its brand even if it exists in a commodity market by providing better quality, value, and most importantly, a unique experience.

DESTINATION BRAND BLUEPRINT

You would never consider constructing a building without the aid of a blueprint. Blueprints are drafted by skilled architects who are practitioners of the profession of creating, designing, and planning all the necessary elements so that you can build things like homes, libraries, or entire office complexes.

The goal is to be recognized as authentic and distinctive. A Brand Blueprint signals what a destination delivers, both in terms of its products and services and its attitude, culture, and the way in which it communicates with its members.

The foundation for the Brand Blueprint, and every brand message and communication, lies in the brand's promise. When an organization utilizes our Brand Blueprint concept, it can expect to optimize the perception of the brand, thus advancing brand equity.

Destinations need a prescribed technique for properly constructing and communicating their brand identity. Just as roundabouts are popular techniques for managing traffic, the BrandAbout defines the key components for a Brand Blueprint.

There are four basic components of our Brand Blueprint as illustrated in Figure 7.10. While traditional marketing practices

FIGURE 7.10

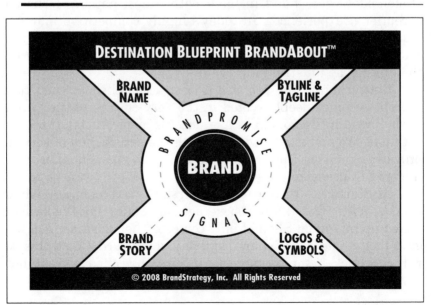

would view these as separate components, our blueprint concept treats them as integral pieces, which comprise one unit. As a total they should strike a harmonious balance that results in creating a synergistic connection with guests, influencers, and stakeholders.

DEVELOPING A DESTINATION'S CULTURE

It feels great when you enter a restaurant or hotel and are greeted with a smile and, "Good morning, sir (or ma'am). May I help you?" Customer service and pleasing a guest or customer should be the number one priority. This applies directly to destinations and how they interact with their guests.

One of the traits of genuine brands is their ability to create a consistent perception based on their transactions with guests. Consistent expectations are usually the result of a strong positive culture that exists within a destination that is focused on making guests, influencers, and stakeholders feel a certain way. Therefore, the culturalization plan should define or fine-tune the correct culture and enhance its positive effect on each guest's, influencer's and stakeholder's experience as reflected by the promise.

Achieving increased loyalty from guests, influencers, and stakeholders goes hand in hand with a destination's focus on exceptional experiences. In today's highly competitive marketplace, it isn't enough to just talk about delivering great service. Successful brands, as the old saying goes, let their actions do the talking, as illustrated in Figure 7.11.

Delivering on the promise is best accomplished when this concept becomes deeply rooted in the very culture of the brand itself. Providing exceptional experiences is inspirational. It begins with a desire and is rewarded through the satisfaction of service providers knowing they are acting in a consistent manner with the brand's promise.

At Starbucks, the customer is first. On a recent visit, when I was ordering five different beverages on a busy day, the barista mixed up my order. She not only corrected her mistake, but she gave them to us free of charge and with a gift card. Could this be why Starbucks remains successful? Sure, the coffee is great, but

FIGURE 7.11

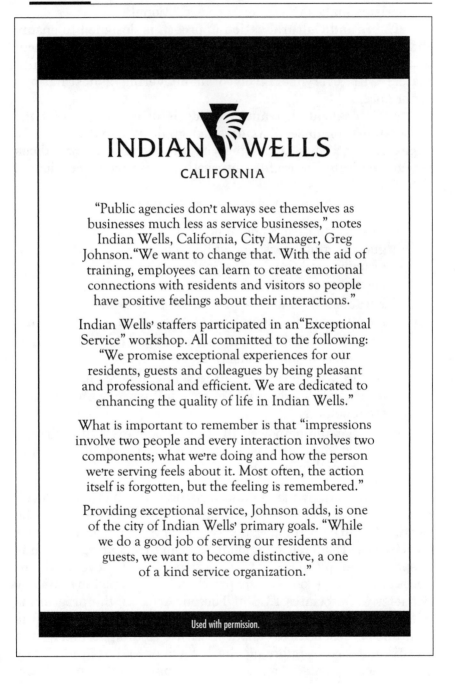

INDIAN WELLS
CALIFORNIA

"Public agencies don't always see themselves as businesses much less as service businesses," notes Indian Wells, California, City Manager, Greg Johnson."We want to change that. With the aid of training, employees can learn to create emotional connections with residents and visitors so people have positive feelings about their interactions."

Indian Wells' staffers participated in an"Exceptional Service" workshop. All committed to the following: "We promise exceptional experiences for our residents, guests and colleagues by being pleasant and professional and efficient. We are dedicated to enhancing the quality of life in Indian Wells."

What is important to remember is that "impressions involve two people and every interaction involves two components; what we're doing and how the person we're serving feels about it. Most often, the action itself is forgotten, but the feeling is remembered."

Providing exceptional service, Johnson adds, is one of the city of Indian Wells' primary goals. "While we do a good job of serving our residents and guests, we want to become distinctive, a one of a kind service organization."

Used with permission.

the feeling you receive not only from the atmosphere but from the baristas makes the experience exceptional.

The Brand Culturalization approach is designed to ensure the accurate delivery of a destination's promise commitment and to enhance the level of understanding of the brand ultimately with everyone involved in delivering a destination's experience.

A culturalization training guide is developed around the destination's promise. This detailed guide is usually 15 to 20 pages in length and is designed as an instructional workbook which facilitates a highly interactive training discussion of three to four hours.

The culturalization plan is used as the basis to:

- Ensure that everyone understands a destination's guests, influencers, and stakeholders' desires, the promise, and the destination's critical goals and objectives.
- Establish a "how to act like a genuine brand" mindset for all associates (employees) involved in a destination.
- Provide real solutions for actual day-to-day situations and improve job satisfaction.
- Inspire associates to want to serve and deliver a destination's promise to guests, influencers, and other stakeholders.
- Engage and empower all associates to excel in their work and create exceptionally positive experiences for guests and influencers.

A new nationwide certification program has been developed to "live the brand" at a destination's frontline level—the Certified Tourism Ambassador (CTA) program. The program's objective is: "To increase regional tourism by inspiring front-line hospitality employees and volunteers to turn every visitor encounter into a positive experience." Developed by Mickey Schaefer & Associates LLC of Tucson, Arizona, the program is highly customized for each destination—not only teaching the frontline representatives about their area's unique history and culture but also reinforcing the behaviors and attitudes they should demonstrate to make an emotional connection with the visitor. It is all about "exceeding customer's expectations in every encounter," according to Schaefer. The Certified Tourism Ambassador program focuses on enhancing the front line's performance and building pride through a lasting culture of quality. It has been implemented in many cities.

The benefits of culturalization can be measured in small assurances or large returns. Exceptional employee morale, increased productivity, enhanced guest loyalty, and a truly distinctive perception by guests are some of the tangible benefits. Successful brands in today's competitive and quickly changing marketplace understand what kind of experience is required. Exceeding service expectations, delivering on a promise, and a reputation for a one-of-a-kind experience can enhance the destination's image.

The following Brand Profile on Tourism Vancouver provides insights into a world-class destination's strategy.

BRAND PROFILE

TOURISM VANCOUVER

DELIVERING ON A DESTINATION PROMISE: VANCOUVER, CANADA[4]

When you think of brand, you often think of consumer goods. Yet destinations need to subscribe to the same principles of strategic branding as consumer goods. In fact, the challenge becomes even greater when you're trying to deliver a destination experience.

When Tourism Vancouver launched its new brand promise and identity in 2005, the goal was simple yet ambitious: to deliver on a commitment of how it wants guests to feel when they visit Vancouver. While visual identity is the face of a brand, its promise is its heart. Following the principles of the Destination BrandScience, the promise was designed as a compass to guide the destination marketing organization, and the broader Vancouver tourism community, in ensuring that it aligned its business activities with a real promise focused on integrity and depth.

In anticipation of an unprecedented decade of opportunity leading up to hosting the 2010 Olympic and Paralympic Winter Games, expansion of the Vancouver Convention and Exhibition Centre, as well as emerging tourism markets, Vancouver knew it was time to do things differently.

FIGURE 7.12

Used with permission.

To clearly express the exuberance of Vancouver, the tourism bureau developed a stylized V in an unexpected four-color palette that represents the city's vitality. In keeping with the focus on the promise, the new identity was launched with a brand story and film to engage the community that needed to deliver on that promise, as well as to ensure community members' understanding of what that promise meant and why it was important to Vancouver's customers. More than ever before, Tourism Vancouver needed to ensure that the brand encapsulated the spectacular natural beauty of the destination and the energetic diversity of its people and experiences. But most importantly Tourism Vancouver needed to ensure that it was relevant to and addressed the needs of the city's diverse customer groups.

Tourism Vancouver now lives and breathes the BrandPromise, knowing that the organization and the Vancouver tourism community must be focused on delivering on the promise to reach the goal of becoming a one-of-a-kind and preferred travel destination. The philosophy: achieve successful delivery of the promise, and tourism growth and success will follow.

Following extensive research with customer groups including independent travelers, meeting planners, and the leisure travel trade, Vancouver's destination BrandPromise was developed:

> The Vancouver experience will exceed visitors' expectations. We will deliver superior value within a spectacular destination that is safe, exciting and welcoming to everyone.

In order to support the tenets of the BrandPromise, Tourism Vancouver has prioritized a number of initiatives and programs:

- *Exceeding expectations* is about delivering a product or service that stands out from anything anyone has experienced before.

  Visitors are the ultimate judges. Vancouver has been voted the Top City in the Americas by readers of *Condé Nast Traveler* magazine for three years running. *Condé Nast Traveler* is highly respected, and its readers are discerning and well traveled. This award is at the top of a long list of accolades that Vancouver has received; these types of designations contribute to Vancouver's goal of being a premier travel destination.

- Providing *superior value* is not simply about cost. It's also about time and feelings: giving people what they want, when they want it and delivering an experience that is positive and memorable.

  To deliver on customer expectations, Tourism Vancouver identified opportunities such as a partnership with Uniglobe Advance Travel to offer inbound air services for convention and meeting delegates, with a value proposition of guaranteed lowest airfares.

- Delivering a *spectacular* destination is not only about physical beauty. It's also about a clean and sustainable environment for the enjoyment of guests and residents.

  Vancouver's natural setting is one of its greatest assets, and it needs to be protected and preserved. Tourism Vancouver has committed to "greening" all of its air travel with the purchase of carbon offset credits through Uniglobe Advance Travel's Green Flight initiative. Tourism Vancouver is the first destination marketing organization to commit to offsetting all its flights through the program. The organization will not only offset flights taken by staff traveling for sales and marketing business but also those flights purchased to bring travel influencer clients, customers, and media to Vancouver. Plus, the opportunity to purchase carbon offset credits will be offered to all convention delegates coming to Vancouver for conferences and meetings, thereby further extending the impact.

- Ensuring the *safety* of its guests is of paramount importance and one of the key factors tourists consider when they're deciding on where to visit.

  In today's travel environment, safety is especially important for travelers. To heighten awareness among frontline tourism staff, a video was developed collectively with the Vancouver Hotel Association, Downtown Vancouver Business Improvement Association, and the Vancouver Police Department. Titled "Customer Service Instinct—Minimizing Property Crime," the objective was to deliver a property crime safety and security training tool to create awareness of how to safeguard visitors' personal belongings by providing scenario-based examples of common property crime techniques and proactive customer service tips for prevention.

- Vancouver is fortunate to boast dozens of festivals, sporting events, world-class attractions, arts and culture product, outdoor recreation, and nightlife, all of which lend credence to positioning it as an *exciting* city.

  Attracting and supporting myriad entertainment options is an integral part of what brings visitors to the city and keeps them coming back. Accordingly, Tourism Vancouver works with numerous festivals and events such as the HSBC Celebration of Light annual fireworks competition, which has a proven history of generating visits to the destination and which has had economic impact. The organization also stages the city's most anticipated event for food lovers—the wildly popular Dine Out Vancouver. This annual culinary promotion invites locals and visitors alike to sample amazing three-course prix-fixe dinners created by Vancouver's exceptional culinary talent over a 17-day period. Making arts product accessible to visitors is fundamental to engaging tourists in a city's cultural life. Operating Tickets Tonight, Vancouver's Community Box Office (a day-of half-price ticket outlet) supports that goal while driving economic return for the cultural community. Building on this work, a new partnership between Tourism Vancouver as the tourism body and the city of Vancouver, outlines the two organizations' commitment to supporting Vancouver's growth toward becoming a vital creative city.

- One of Vancouver's goals is to be North America's most accessible city. That's part of the destination's promise to be *welcoming* to everyone. And that commitment extends to people of every ethnic origin, religion, and lifestyle.

  As the tourism industry leader, that means investing in targeted segment marketing, including creative campaigns such as offering a Win Your Wedding Sweepstakes in Vancouver targeting the U.S.-based gay and lesbian market. It also means developing capabilities in offering meaningful translated collateral communications and Web sites for various cultures such as the emerging Chinese market.

Building a brand is about delivering on a promise and requires an entire tourism community to fulfill that commitment in order to become a one-of-a-kind premier travel destination. Travel is a great instigator. Its propensity to educate, to generate new ways of thinking, and to help people shed cultural prejudice is what it's all about. Tourism Vancouver's responsibility is to contribute to making Vancouver what the world should be: a model of urban civility, cultural diversity, environmental respect, and compassion for the less fortunate members of society. It is also about inviting visitors to a place where a community of hosts can welcome the world with pride and where each guest is a guest of everyone who calls Vancouver home.

THOUGHT GUIDE

COMMUNITY BRANDS: THE DESTINATION BRANDPROMISE

- Community brands are the result of a partnership among leaders to develop a destination that is preferred for tourism, economic development, and business growth and investment.
- A tourism strategy should answer the following questions:
  - What should our destination's distinctive promise be?
  - What does our destination stand for in the minds of the key stakeholders?
  - What BrandPromise experience should be communicated by our tourism representatives to our current and potential guests, influencers, and stakeholders?
  - Are we dedicated to providing an exceptional experience for every guest?

- ○ What is the consensus regarding the optimum brand image and future position for our destination?
- ○ What is the most effective way to use marketing, advertising, and communications to gain competitive advantage and increase our destination's success?
- ○ What is the first word that we want to come to mind when prospective guests and influencers think of our destination?
- ○ What brand attributes are important to our destination's varied stakeholders?
- When a destination thinks and acts like a genuine brand, the entire community understands what the promise is and how they can deliver the right experience.
- A slogan or an advertising tagline is not a strategy.
- A destination culturalization plan is used as a basis to:
  - ○ Ensure that everyone understands a destination's guests', influencers', and stakeholders' desires, the BrandPromise, and the organization's critical goals and objectives.
  - ○ Establish a "how to act like a genuine brand" mindset for all associates (employees).
  - ○ Provide real solutions for actual day-to-day situations and improve job satisfaction.
  - ○ Inspire tourism associates to want to serve and deliver a destination's promise to guests, influencers, and other stakeholders.
  - ○ Engage and empower all associates to excel in their work and create exceptionally positive experiences for guests, influencers, and other stakeholders.

CHAPTER **8**

Personal Brands

Great stars may be born, but it's the celebrities who embrace the principles of BrandScience that enjoy long term brand success.

THINKING ABOUT YOUR BRAND

All people have a personal brand identity, whether they like it or not. It may be as simple as how you are perceived by your wife, husband, or partner. Or it could be as complex as the brand identity of an actor, sports star, or politician. Whether you are a doctor, lawyer, actor, athlete, or minister, the principles of BrandScience apply to you. In fact, these principles apply to us all in every aspect of our lives regardless of position or accomplishment. It is all about how you want to be perceived, and every person is a brand to some extent.

People can choose to ignore the BrandScience principles, or they can embrace them to enhance their happiness and success. It's just like the volume on your radio or iPod; you can turn up the volume or mute your brand as you desire.

There is a "science" to creating and building successful brands as evidenced by the widespread success of brands that have applied the BrandMindset philosophy. The business world has discovered the BrandScience principles and how to apply them for maximum success.

What does this have to do with an individual, an average person who is not in business, per se? Each of us is affected

FIGURE 8.1

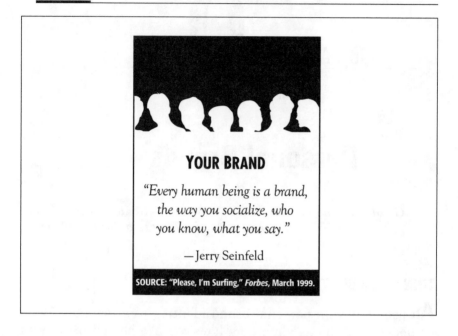

YOUR BRAND

"*Every human being is a brand,
the way you socialize, who
you know, what you say.*"

—Jerry Seinfeld

SOURCE: "Please, I'm Surfing," *Forbes*, March 1999.

every day by the perceptions of others. How other people treat
you depends, in part, on their perceptions of you. Any person can
now utilize the proven techniques and methodologies that have
been used by the corporate world to create powerful and successful brands. You don't need to be a celebrity or be wealthy,
or famous.

So what's the secret to enhancing the perceptions of your
personal brand? First of all, you have to care. If you don't care
about how other people perceive you, then the concept of a personal brand is not for you. Second, it's essential that you make
a promise related to how you want others to feel when they
come in contact with you. It's probably obvious, but you have
to act and behave in a manner that affirms others and creates
certain emotional and functional perceptions. Regardless of
whether you're a professional athlete, teacher, or stay-at-home
mom or dad, these principles apply on a relative basis. It's
never too soon to work on your brand. Successful personal
brand development should begin before you become famous—
not after.

Peter Montoya, author of *The Brand Called You*, maintains that Tiger Woods, Oprah Winfrey, and Charles Schwab "had a vision of where they wanted to go, and an instinctive understanding that to get there, they had to represent something clear and beneficial in people's minds."[1]

You need to ask yourself whether you want to be admired, respected, or appreciated—by anyone. If your answer is no, then you can stop reading. If your answer is yes, then as they say, "Let the games begin."

You may ask, if this is a science, then why are there so many examples of failed brands—per-

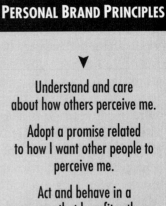

PERSONAL BRAND PRINCIPLES

▼

Understand and care about how others perceive me.

Adopt a promise related to how I want other people to perceive me.

Act and behave in a manner that benefits others and affirms my promise.

sonal and business alike? As we discussed in Chapter 3, it has a lot to do with the feel/do law. Most people think that if they do something well, such as make a lot of money or become an exceptional athlete, the right brand perceptions will happen naturally. Unfortunately, if a person does not focus on the feelings of others and how they want to be perceived, that person will find it difficult or impossible to achieve genuine brand status.

Just because people are successful or well known doesn't mean that they get expert brand advice. When famous people get into trouble, they are usually getting legal advice on how to minimize or control a problem. Rarely do they receive qualified celebrity brand advice, because rarely do they have a strategy for their brand. The accepted mindset has been that any publicity is good publicity and that controversy is always good.

Times have changed, and now it's very important to think carefully about what you do and how you are perceived. While pride may keep them from admitting it, I believe that when celebrities or athletes get into trouble, it costs them an enormous amount of money and personal trauma. If there's any doubt, would any of them like to experience their last controversy again? I think not.

Things happen to people every day. "It's always something," meaning that you may not be able to avoid ever having a "bad" day or difficult situation, but it's what you do about it that makes the difference. If you have a plan for how you want to be perceived, you're going to be way ahead of others who become a pinball in the machine of life.

The reality is that most of the time celebrities or athletes who become famous are keen to become more famous. Rarely do they decide what their personal promise is, what their personal brand should stand for, and how they want to be perceived. Imagine a framed picture of a celebrity who has damaged his or her personal brand with a caption that reads, she knew a lot about acting but nothing about her "brand."

The same situation applies to any ordinary person as well. It's easy to get overwhelmed by the pace of everyday life and to lose sight of how to manage personal brand perceptions.

CARING ABOUT PERCEPTIONS

Regardless of your situation, the first step is to understand how others feel about you. I remember the first time I experienced a 360-degree performance evaluation in corporate life. I was petrified by the idea that people who worked with me at all levels in the corporation would be evaluating me. Traditionally, executives reviewed the performance of the people that worked directly "for" them. A 360-degree review includes all of the people that work "with" an executive.

However, I soon realized that the issue was not really about how I was rated (as long as it wasn't too bad); it was really about how I reacted to the evaluations. It, of course, was a wonderful opportunity to improve and focus on how I wanted other people to feel as opposed to just "getting the job done."

This is the same technique that anyone can employ to evaluate his or her personal brand perceptions in the minds of others. It begins with asking yourself and then other people (friends, colleagues, etc.) for their perceptions of you. The secret in this is to focus on people's feelings.

You first have to evaluate yourself before you can ask others. It's important to put a stake in the ground as to where you think you're perceived by others. Following are a few questions to begin a personal Brand Assessment. Of course, you can create your own questions or change the attributes in these questions.

Personal Brand Assessment Questions

- What's the first word or phrase that comes to mind when you think of me?
- On a scale of 1 to 10 where 10 is exceptional, answer the following:
  - How distinct am I?
  - How charming am I?
  - How happy am I?
  - How creative am I?
  - How energetic am I?
  - How inspiring am I?
  - How thoughtful am I?
  - How outgoing am I?
  - How good am I at what I do?
  - How intelligent am I?

    In addition to the questions about personal attributes, you might also ask:
- How would you describe my personal style? What kind of car would I be?
- What am I really good at?
- In what areas could I improve?

One might ask, how scientific is the process of asking a few friends, acquaintances, or colleagues these questions. The answer, it doesn't really matter. People may be hesitant to tell you the real truth; however, it will still be directionally helpful. You can take a personality test if you want more scientific information, or you can retain an executive coach.

The concept of developing your personal brand applies to any leader in industry or the nonprofit world, according to Tom Waldron, executive coach and CEO of Waldron & Company. Waldron & Company, a leader in human resources consulting, works closely with senior-level executives to align their perceptions with their organization's goals. Unlike celebrities and sports figures, executives are normally not subject to media attention, so their brand is more under their control.

Tom explains, "We begin by asking the executive the following questions: What is the legacy you would like to leave, looking three to five years into the future? What will people say about their experience with you as a leader? Specifically, how will the board of directors, CEO, peers, and staff describe you? As an example, with staff, we may ask what people will say about your impact on their environment and culture. What did they learn from you? How did you contribute as a leader? Were you trusted?" Once these questions are answered, then a personal plan can be developed to achieve the appropriate impressions.

The key is to compare your own assessment with those of others and any other input you have and then decide—who do you want to be? And how do you want to be perceived? As Al Ries, a much respected marketing consultant and author, says, "Your role is to make the changes necessary to create a better perception."[2]

If you are famous already or an established celebrity or sports hero, then the research component is much more comprehensive, and it is outlined in the celebrity section of this chapter.

Once you have created a perceptual map of how you are perceived and how you desire to be perceived, then you are ready to take the next step.

WHAT'S YOUR PERSONAL PROMISE?

As you think about your personal promise, it doesn't have to be about being powerful, rich, or famous. Your promise is about how you want to be described and how you would like other people to feel about. (See Figure 8.2.)

A good exercise is to think about people whom you like or admire and make a list of their attributes or behaviors that you respect. Make a list of the positive attributes from several people and a list of the behaviors you don't like. Select four attributes that you would like to be associated with. Reflecting on the Brand Balance we discussed in Chapter 3, it would be great to pick two emotional attributes and two functional attributes. (See Figure 8.3.)

FIGURE 8.2

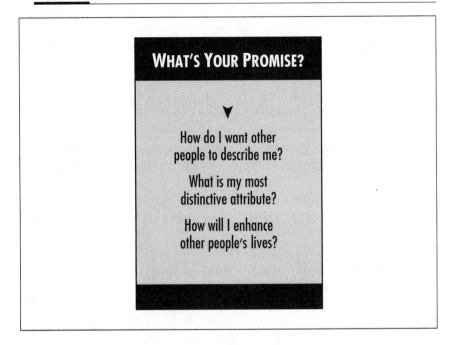

FIGURE 8.3

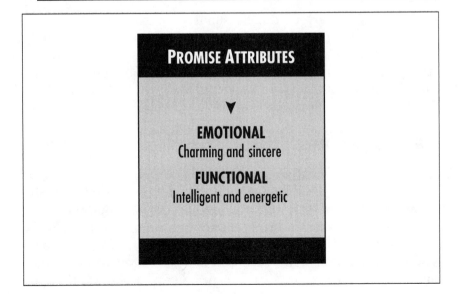

Another essential step in developing a personal promise is to select someone you admire as a role model. This provides a tangible inspiration to help you plan your own success. It's also important to realize that you will be a role model for others, and so you must be willing to accept that opportunity and responsibility.

The important thing is to decide how you want to be perceived. You may choose to focus on certain attributes at home and others at work. However, there can be a risk of the Dr. Jekyll and Mr. Hyde syndrome. Your promise should be who you want to be, and it should be reflected in how others describe you in the future. The most important thing to remember is that you have a choice.

I was in the process of moving to accept a new job, and one of my friends asked me, "How do you want to be perceived in the new company?" Without thinking, I said, "the same way I am perceived now." It was the first time in my life that I realized that I had the option to decide who I wanted to be and not just be a continuation of my past.

When you have decided how you want others to describe you, you can begin to think about your distinctive trait. The three aspects of your promise (Figure 8.2) are designed to be like the peeling an onion—layer after layer after layer. You can apply these a little or a lot depending on the depth you want to take your promise to.

The third part of the personal promise focuses on your interest in enhancing other people's lives. While this might sound as though it is a "values" discussion, it is not meant to be. It's up to you to become who you want to be. The more robust a promise becomes, the more impact it has on your life.

LIVING YOUR PROMISE

Consistent with our discussion of brand throughout this book is the concept that a personal brand is about being real and genuine, not hype or a public relations exercise. Whatever your promise is, it's essential that you act in a manner that's consistent with your promise. Your promise is personal; it's never something you brag about. The test is whether you are perceived in a manner consistent with your promise and not just that you

FIGURE 8.4

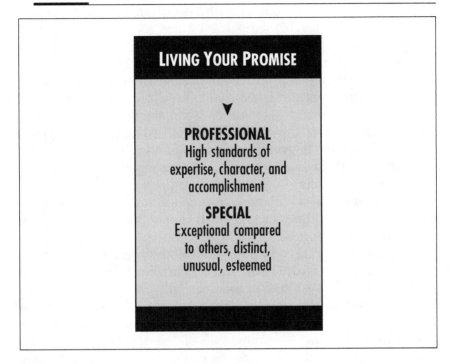

have a promise. In other words, if you don't act consistently with your promise, effectively you don't have one.

Having a promise doesn't mean that you're now perfect or that you will not break your promise or that you will not have challenges or problems. Your promise is your guiding light, and the idea is to be as true to your promise as you can be.

We have selected two attributes—professional and special (exceptional)—from dozens of possibilities to use as examples of the importance of living your promise. (See Figure 8.4.)

Professional

It could be said that people should be *professional*, regardless of what they do. *Professional* could refer to someone with an extensive understanding, education, or years of experience related to a specific area of expertise. Being perceived as a professional certainly includes a functional requirement that people "know what they are doing." Someone who is a professional should be functionally capable of doing his or her job well; so we will accept that as a given. However, I think there are more important requirements to being perceived as professional, and those have to do with how a professional makes other people feel.

Professional athletes get paid for what amateurs do for free, but this does not necessarily mean they are professionals in the true sense of the word. Real professionals of any type— celebrity, athlete, lawyer, whatever—should be admired and respected for all their actions and behaviors and are indeed perceived as professional in every sense of the word.

In order to be perceived as a professional, it's necessary to exhibit a certain character and spirit that separates real professionals from the unprofessionals.

Bruce Blomgren of Indian Wells, California, is a respected real estate broker with Dyson and Dyson. He is widely regarded as the top real estate agent in the Coachella Valley (Palm Springs and surrounding areas). His list of high-profile clientele is as impressive as his list of accomplishments. He was ranked by the *Wall Street Journal* as number 33 of the top 200 real estate agents in the nation. Since 1998 he has participated in over $530 million in transactions. He is the consummate professional.

What is the secret to this success? It's really not a secret. Bruce is "just himself." He is consistent and dedicated to his authentic self, which translates to customer satisfaction and trust. When he says he is going to do something, he does it. If small mistakes are made, he takes them seriously, as a mistake compromises his integrity.

Client perception is paramount, and it easily translates to the bottom line. Bruce has assembled a team of professionals, and he makes certain that his colleagues and team members embrace his promise. Bruce is able to focus on how he wants his clients to feel. Renowned for his one-on-one brand of attention, Bruce anticipates his clients' needs and exceeds their expectations.

When asked if he consciously created a brand, Bruce indicated that it evolved as he observed the importance of keeping his promises. In other words, being a professional is not just people's expertise, it's, more importantly, their character and their way of doing business.

Of course, Bruce knows his business and is highly respected for his real estate expertise. However, his expertise is not solely what makes him a one-of-a-kind personal brand; it's his down-to-earth nature coupled with his authentic approach to customer satisfaction that make it possible for others to perceive him as a professional and that have earned him many referrals and recommendations. But mostly it is respect that is the foundation of his real estate consulting business.

Special

The second personal attribute we're focusing on is *special*. Having others describe you as being *special* in a positive way or your focus on making other people feel special could both be relevant.

Being described as a special person or someone who's held in esteem by others is a great quality. It's important to note that to be deemed special depends on others' impressions. People confuse awareness or being famous as a requirement for being special, when in actuality it's a person's distinctive or exceptional traits that are really more important. To be held in high esteem does not require a person to be famous. It can be achieved by anyone who focuses on his genuine attributes as interpreted by his circle of friends, business associates, or those in his social environment.

In Northern Louisiana, the Brazil plantation's cook, Cora Turner, crafted and slowbrewed her sweet barbecue sauce incorporating only the best and freshest ingredients and a "pinch of lovin'." Since 1937, the Turner family has kept Cora's secret recipe alive to continue the tradition of "original Louisiana Bar-B-Que."

JT's Original Bar-B-Que Company is still a family business managed by James and Elsie Turner. The Turners believe that "authentic Bar-B-Que in the tradition of America's Southern plantations is truly a spiritual experience . . . something very special."

When you enjoy the unique flavor of their sauce or Bar-B-Que at their restaurant, their distinct and exceptional flavors come alive, but most of all it's their passion that sets them apart.

FIGURE 8.5

Used with permission.

In order to be perceived as special, a personal brand needs to be real and authentic.

CELEBRITY BRAND PHILOSOPHY

As we discussed earlier, you do not have to be famous or a celebrity to apply the principles of Personal BrandScience. If someone is already a celebrity or has the desire to become famous or a celebrity, then, as they say, "You'll have to raise the bar."

World-class professionals, celebrities, and individuals who desire to optimize how they are perceived—their image and success—must become personally involved in the process of building their brand. It cannot be delegated to someone else—an agent or public relations firm.

A successful individual who desires to build a celebrity brand must think like a "genuine celebrity brand," and this requires a different mindset, perspective, and strategy from business as usual. Successful individuals need to be perceived as distinctive and make a promise to deliver emotional and functional benefits.

As Mark Steinberg says, "People try to create brands out of individuals who are not really committed to be a brand, and unfortunately, it's going to catch up with them." Mark should know; he is the senior vice president and global managing director of Golf for IMG, the sports and entertainment powerhouse. He also personally represents Tiger Woods and Annika Sorenstam. He also points out that to become a genuine celebrity brand requires a "promise and commitment to yourself, sport, work ethic, and character to become the person you want to be."

When people think and act like a genuine celebrity brand, everyone who is associated with them understands what their promise is and how they deliver the right experience. Celebrities or successful individuals may be involved in a variety of business interests, and they must become actively involved in developing the strategy for their brand. It's important that each of those businesses and related brands deliver the right promise to their respective constituents. An individual's related enterprises must provide exceptional customer satisfaction for long-term success. The key for an individual to become a successful genuine brand is to focus on providing distinctive and relevant experiences that provide lasting and memorable impressions in all of his or her business-related activities. Genuine celebrity brands make a promise, and they deliver on that promise consistently, eagerly, and at the customer's convenience. The power of a promise is based on how people feel toward the brand.

Robert Tyre Jones Jr., popularly known as Bobby Jones, was one of the greatest golfers in the world. Clearly, his golf ability was world class; however, it was his demeanor and character that made him a genuine celebrity brand.

Bobby Jones wrote the following in 1967 for the Augusta National Golf Club:

> In golf, customs of etiquette and decorum are just as important as rules governing play. It is appropriate for spectators to applaud successful strokes in proportion to difficulty but excessive demonstrations by a player or his partisans are not proper because of

the possible effect upon other competitors. Most distressing to those who love the game of golf is applauding or cheering of misplays or misfortunes of a player. Such occurrences have been rare at the Masters, but we must eliminate them entirely if our patrons are to continue to merit their reputation as the most knowledgeable and considerate in the world.[3]

Bobby Jones's personal style made him distinctive in every way. Louise Suggs was one of the charter members of the Ladies Professional Golf Association (LPGA) and dominated women's golf in the late 1940s and throughout the 1950s with 58 professional victories, including 11 major championships. Louise, who was nicknamed Little Miss Sluggs by Bob Hope, had the distinct pleasure of knowing Bobby Jones when she was learning to play golf. She describes him as, "Always the Southern gentleman; he was an icon and not just in golf." She watched Bobby play a lot, and it really helped her develop her style. Once he told Louise, "Knock the hell out of it … it will come down somewhere."

When you listen to people who knew Bobby Jones, they always hold him in high esteem. It's easy to see why when you watch his golf instruction videos. His personal charm and sincerity were never overwhelmed by his intelligence or accomplishments.

Many individuals become famous for their sports ability, acting talent, public service, politics, and the like. The few who achieve genuine brand status have demonstrated an understanding that to be perceived as truly "authentic" requires a unique mindset. It's not just about success, fame, or money; it's about achieving a balance between the fame and being perceived as a genuine person who is real and respected, not just some kind of a star.

Whether or not a famous person or an athlete can become a genuine celebrity brand depends on many factors. One of them being, is this person brandable? "You have to be good enough at something that someone really cares about," says Charlie Mechem, an esteemed corporate advisor and personal advisor to many celebrities, including Arnold Palmer and Annika Sorenstam. As the chairman emeritus of the Ladies Professional Golf Association, he has had a lot of firsthand experience in the celebrity business.

If indeed people believe they are brandable, based on talent and accomplishments, then they will need to focus on becoming perceived as unique in a positive way. There are so many talented people in every walk of life that being really good at what you do is only the entry fee.

It's absolutely necessary to focus on your values, character, and what you believe in. As Louise Suggs says, you have to have the right "basics" related to your talent as well as your personal life.

Many famous people believe it's their right or obligation to tell other people how they should think, act, or behave. They say it's their right, as in free speech. Unfortunately, this is a serious problem, since there is no such thing as "free speech." The Constitution of the United States respects "freedom of speech"; however, there are consequences whenever an individual speaks. People who desire to be genuine brands should always focus on being known for what they support in a positive way rather than what they are against.

In order to become a genuine celebrity brand, a person needs to focus on being:

- Good enough at what he or she does so that other people will really care.
- Perceived as a unique, one-of-a-kind individual and on being identified with positives, such as the kinds of beliefs that affirm others.

The desire to be a genuine celebrity brand begins with the enthusiasm and excitement of a star combined with the grace and charm of a real person.

BUILDING A CELEBRITY BRAND IS HARD WORK

It's easy to admire celebrities' lifestyles and the benefits of being rich and famous or both. However, successful celebrities' personal work schedules, social demands, and the nature of being famous add up to really hard work and lots of personal sacrifices.

Greg Norman

Mention the words "the shark," and many people will correctly think of Greg Norman. Although he became famous playing professional golf, his Great White Shark Enterprises provides a good lesson in how celebrities and famous athletes can build successful brands. He has consistently used the "shark" word and shark-related images throughout his business enterprises to reinforce his brand equity.

Greg Norman is actively involved in all of his brand ventures, and "he just has a really amazing business acumen," says Suzy Biszantz, CEO and president of the Greg Norman clothing line.[4] "It's very natural to him. Our customers are always so surprised that unlike many professional athletes he's so in tune with our business and their business."[5]

Great White Shark Enterprises is a multinational corporation with hundreds of employees, partnerships, and licensing agreements. It is involved in golf course design, apparel, wines, and residential real estate development. According to Bryan Moss, president of Gulfstream (private jets), "He's one of those rare individuals where you can take his word or handshake to the bank."[6]

Greg Norman has been very successful in business and in the business of building his family of brands. He is involved in every aspect of his business from tasting his wine to each detail of a development site.[7] "My site visits are a little intense because I've got to see everything so I just put on my boots and go."[8]

In his book, *The Way of the Shark*, he tells the story of his friend teaching him the science of "DIN and DIP"—do it now and do it proper. Even if you don't like doing something, you've got to do it anyway. He also believes in three principles:

> The next minute is the most important minute of your life.
> You are limited only by your own imagination.
> Your dreams are the blueprints of reality.[9]

Rachael Ray

She's everywhere! Whether it's a bookstore, supermarket, or kitchen retailer, she's smiling at you from every corner. Her self-deprecating wit, down-to-earth appeal, and hyperenergetic approach combine to make her a celebrity powerhouse.

However, she did not get her celebrity status from a Hollywood plot. She earned it the old-fashioned way. Rachael was born in Cape Cod and grew up in the Adirondacks working at her family's restaurants and later working in specialty grocery stores in New York City and Albany, New York. While in Albany, she noticed that the prepared food sold well but that basic groceries did not. After failing to persuade local chefs to teach 30-minute cooking classes, Ray did it herself. They became so popular that a local TV station put her on camera. "I'd serve wine on the sly and play theme music," she says. "It was just a huge party."[10]

The rest, as they say, is history. She has become a Food Network star with numerous cookbooks that have sold millions of copies (she has a new book titled *Just in Time*, which was published in November 2007), and the *Rachael Ray* show, coproduced by her friend and mentor Oprah Winfrey, has become a daytime hit. She's influencing everyone by providing recipes for NASA's astronauts and influencing corporate America to send their employees to cooking seminars to improve their management and interpersonal skills. As the *New York Times* reports, "The cooking class approach to corporate team building has caught on."[11]

Rachael isn't afraid to be real, and she loves having fun. "'Share' is my favorite word,"[12] she says, and here are a few recommendations for things to share from her magazine, *Every Day with Rachael Ray*:

- Smiles with people passing on the street
- Time with someone who might be lonely
- Good thoughts with people you love
- A great joke
- Your 300-plus thread count sheets[13]

She works very hard, writing all her own recipes. Typical days start very early in the morning as she deals with endless interviews, photo shoots, and meetings. "I feel like an ox at the end of the day ... I like working hard."[14] It's easy to see why people connect with Rachael's personal warmth, sincerity, and never-ending energy.

One thing that most successful celebrities have in common is that they love what they do, and they work hard. However, even working hard does not guarantee a successful brand. The key to building a genuine celebrity brand is to follow a disciplined, proven process which is outlined in the following sections of this chapter.

CELEBRITY BRAND ASSESSMENT

The process of creating a genuine celebrity brand is consistent with the recommendations outlined in the previous pages of this chapter, only a much more in-depth commitment is necessary. As we discussed earlier, the first step is the Brand Assessment exercise. There are many existing assessment methodologies that should be considered in developing a strategy and promise for a celebrity brand. Some of these are listed in Figure 8.6.

The influence of a celebrity in terms of product endorsements and overall equity is best determined by measurement and empirical data, according to Don Morgan, senior partner at GMA Research Corporation. With this in mind, there are several methods that can be used to assess the overall strength and equity of a celebrity brand. It should be noted that a professional celebrity brand assessment would include a comprehensive image and equity evaluation utilizing multiple research methodologies.

FIGURE 8.6

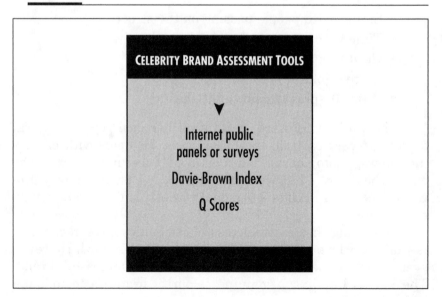

There are syndicated measurement services available that regularly measure celebrities for their overall brand power based on selected attributes and variables (i.e., appeal, influence, trust, etc.). These are listed in Figure 8.7. The most recent system, called the Davie-Brown index (DBI), was introduced in 2006 by Davie-Brown Entertainment. This measurement is based on individual attributes and a combination of variables that are used to evaluate celebrities in a number of categories: sports, entertainment, politics, business, and so on. Based on a national panel of 1.5 million consumers, the DBI includes data for more than 1,500 celebrity brands. Oprah Winfrey and Tom Hanks are ranked among the highest. While the highest DBI aggregate score is 100, both Winfrey and Hanks score in the 95 and above percentile—very rarefied air. Close behind though

FIGURE 8.7

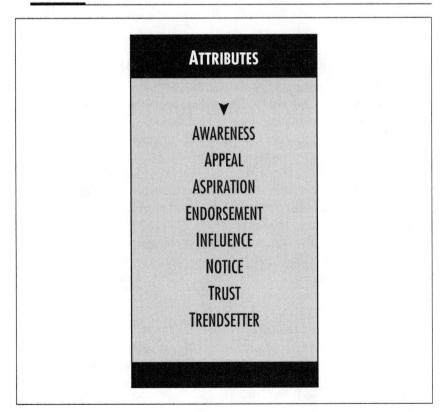

ATTRIBUTES

▼

AWARENESS

APPEAL

ASPIRATION

ENDORSEMENT

INFLUENCE

NOTICE

TRUST

TRENDSETTER

are Bill Cosby, Michael Jordan, and Tiger Woods. Many other celebrities have high awareness scores based on their publicity and notoriety, but they score low on trust and relevance, so their overall rankings based on the DBI are lower. The DBI scores measure the attributes listed in Figure 8.7 and can be helpful in evaluating a celebrity for product endorsements or as a spokesperson.

DBI data are available in a variety of custom reports which evaluate a celebrity overall and compare a celebrity with other celebrities within a particular group. For example, if a celebrity is a professional athlete, he or she can be compared to other celebrities in that same category as well as overall. A single DBI report is priced at about $1,000; multiple customized reports increase the price.

The DBI produces regular reports, so a tracking system can be established to measure and monitor changes in a celebrity's brand impact on consumers' perceptions, the brand image, and trends.

Another commonly used celebrity brand score is known as the "Q score" which was established over 40 years ago by Marketing Evaluations/TvQ. According to Nike spokesman Rodney Knox, "the Q scores system is well known in the sports marketing world; it helps us to make sure we're choosing the correct athletes to endorse our products."[15]

The Q rating scores are based on two factors: the public's familiarity with a celebrity and how much they like or dislike the person. Q scores have historically been used in the entertainment and media industries to measure the strength or marketability of television actors and on-air newscasters as well as professional athletes. However, they are now being employed in a number of applications including deceased celebrities to measure their potential influence. In general, the higher the Q rating, the more desirable the celebrity is to a network or movie producer.

BrandStrategy and GMA Research conduct celebrity brand assessments on a customized basis. Typically the assessment involves a national online survey panel of consumers that rates celebrities on selected attributes through a questionnaire. The survey includes variables such as celebrity brand awareness, relevance, trust, purchase influence, integrity and reliability, role model, and work ethic as well as other factors. By asking consumers to rate the celebrity brand on these attributes using rating scales, a brand index can be created. Going a little further, we can ask consumers what a celebrity brand stands for in order to determine if their association is in line with how the celebrity wants to be perceived compare to and the public's perceptions of whether the celebrity's status is improving, staying the same, or in decline. Online surveys are a very efficient methodology and cost-effective tool for assessing celebrity brands.

GMA Research conducts proprietary surveys for BrandStrategy, Inc.'s celebrity clients. It also combines all the perceptions of syndicated surveys with the proprietary research to prepare a brand assessment report.

The key to a successful celebrity assessment is to evaluate and compare a wide variety of images and perceptions in order to create a perceptual map. This perceptual map outlines key attribute performance measures so that a comprehensive strategy can be created for a celebrity brand.

THE POWER OF A REAL PROMISE

People who are famous and understand the BrandPromise methodology enhance their chances for success. This is especially important for those celebrities who have become involved or invested in a variety of business ventures. The concept of making a real promise is a fundamental success factor for celebrities and their business investors. When you experience a celebrity's promise, you can really tell the difference.

Craig and Kathryn Hall would easily qualify as famous. Craig is a true self-made entrepreneur who started in business at the young age of 10 to become the author of five books and the founder of a multibillion dollar investment firm. And he received the Horatio Alger Award. Kathryn Hall was a successful corporate lawyer who acquired her interest in the wine business from her father, and she was the U.S. ambassador to Austria from 1999 to 2001. Together they are developing their winery into a genuine brand that is destined to become a wine country landmark.

FIGURE 8.8

Reprinted with permission.

Many successful individuals have become involved in the wine business, but for Kathryn and Craig it is much more than another hobby; it's a real passion. Beginning with Sacrashe Vineyard in the Rutherford appellation of Napa Valley, they now own and manage over 3,300 acres with 500 acres being planted in vineyards. Their new Frank Gehry designed visitors center for wine tasting, hospitality, and retail sales will serve as a focal point for creating a one-of-a-kind experience that "celebrates life." Craig and Kathryn Hall are collectors of contemporary art and greatly admire the work of Frank Gehry, who believes that "architecture is art." His sculptural approach to architecture is best seen in his most famous work, the Guggenheim Museum in Bilbao, Spain, as well as the Walt Disney Concert Hall in Los Angeles.

While they certainly are focused on growing and making fine wines, as Kathryn says, "We are in the wine business to inspire the senses and celebrate life." Everything they do is about creating an experience for others that fulfills that promise.

Hopefully, it's obvious by now that before a genuine celebrity brand can be developed, a very personal question must be answered: What's your promise? The brand profile for Annika Sorenstam outlines the approach to the development of a successful celebrity brand.

BRAND PROFILE

ANNIKA SORENSTAM

Growing up as a little girl in Sweden, Annika Sorenstam always dreamed about playing professional golf on the LPGA tour. One day she called her father to pick her up at the driving range on a rainy afternoon. When he arrived, he saw other kids continuing to practice as the rain poured down. As they drove away, Annika recalls her father saying; "You know Annika, there are no shortcuts to success." Her father made that statement 23 years and 69 LPGA wins ago, and Annika says, "It still inspires me to this day."

BRAND FOCUS

When you meet Annika in person, it's very clear that she is interested in you. She looks you straight in your eyes with a sincerity and interest that confirms that she is pursuing her dream. Her golf accomplishments are legendary, but it's her focus and dedication to her brand that is at the heart of what a genuine celebrity brand is all about.

Most professional athletes who have accomplished significant success are usually not knowledgeable in the science of building a personal brand. Brand-related activities are usually delegated by celebrities to their agents, business managers, or public relations staff. Annika has followed a different path. For several years, she has been reading and studying other brand successes and observing how other exceptional celebrities have built their personal brands.

FIGURE 8.9

Used with permission.

PROFESSIONAL PERSPECTIVE

Annika's quest began with the formation of an advisory board of successful CEOs and experts to provide world-class expertise and knowledge and to guide her strategy for her brand. However, she is intimately involved in every detail and activity of her brand.

A key factor in celebrities' plans for their brand is to create an advisory board of successful executives and experts that is involved for the long term, not just for the current "deal." Another factor for success is for the celebrities to "be in charge of their brand," not be mere participants; after all it is their personal brand.

Annika made the commitment to develop a long-term strategy for her brand and commissioned an independent assessment of her perceptions and image. The personal Brand Assessment provided her with an objective view of her brand's perceptions in the minds of the public, corporate executives, and industry influencers. The research provided a list of attributes that could be used to plan and measure her future brand activities. Annika's team could then evaluate and review all her images, perceptions, and activities compared to her desired attributes.

THE BRAND BLUEPRINT

After the completion of the Brand Assessment, Annika and her team began to consider what kind of visual brand representations she wanted to be associated with in her future activities. Her decision was to create a "branded family" based on one word—Annika. This strategy was consistent with the science of one-word celebrity brands such as Seinfeld, Oprah, and the like. It also worked well because of her unique name and the balance of the letter A that frames her name. The original "ANNIKA" concept was used by Cutter & Buck for her apparel brand. James Clark, president of James Clark Design in Seattle, developed the concept into a comprehensive Brand Blueprint (Figure 8.11).

Each and every one of Annika's enterprises and sponsor activities follows her graphic design guide, which ensures the

FIGURE 8.10

ANNIKA SORENSTAM

Annika is the greatest female golfer of our generation, and often regarded as the best player in LPGA history. Her prestigious list of accomplishments includes her 2003 induction into the LPGA and World Halls of Fame, ten major championships, 85 worldwide professional victories, eight LPGA Player of the Year awards, and participation on seven Solheim Cup teams.

In 2001 Annika earned the nickname "Miss 59" when she became the first female to break 60 in an official LPGA tournament. Through her success she has transcended the game of golf, as evidenced by the numerous "Female Athlete of the Year" awards she has received around the world. Annika literally holds more than one third of all LPGA records, and her work ethic and dedication to both golf and fitness is truly legendary. She is the first woman to appear on the cover of Golf Digest in nearly 30 years.

FIGURE 8.11

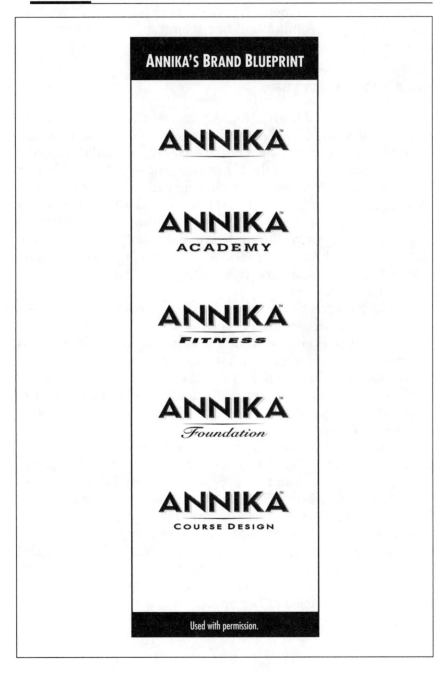

consistent development and use of her brand. As James Clark described his involvement, "It was a real pleasure to work in partnership with Annika and her team and to experience her creativity and passion."

BRINGING HER BRAND TO LIFE

For the past two decades, Annika has worked to master her skills in the game of golf as well as the methods that allow her body and mind to reach their utmost potential. As she perfected her approach with the help of her two coaches, Henri Reis and Kai Fusser, she dreamed about sharing her passion for golf and fitness. Through the unveiling of the ANNIKA Academy, her vision has become a reality. This "boutique" school caters to small groups by providing individualized golf instruction and custom-designed fitness programs. This unique concept, state-of-the-art facility, and luxurious setting create a truly amazing experience.

In all her brand enterprises, Annika strives to inspire others to reach their optimum level of success and fulfillment.

She wants everyone who is associated with her business enterprises to understand what her promise is and how to deliver the right experience. It is important to her that each of her businesses and related brands deliver the right promise of inspirational experiences. The ANNIKA Academy's promise is outlined in Figure 8.12.

Annika wants her brand to be distinctive and to provide lasting and memorable impressions. She knows that the power of a promise is based on how people feel toward her brand.

Annika is closely associated with her championship golf. However, as she began to create the strategy for her brand, it was necessary to communicate that she has a wide range of interests including course and clothing design and culinary and philanthropic activities. When people picture her in their minds, it was necessary that they expand their visual images of her to reflect the many facets of her brand.

FIGURE 8.12

SPONSORS WHO ARE PARTNERS

When celebrities have a strategy for their brand, it provides a roadmap for everyone to follow. The best situation is when celebrities and their sponsors share the same values. Annika's team created a brand guide as the result of her initial strategy, which outlines every aspect of her brand from A to Z and which is the key to a partnership with her sponsors. It is constantly updated and provides the direction for all involved to accomplish their mutual goals. Her sponsors include Callaway Golf, Cutter & Buck, Ginn, *Golf Digest* (*Golf for Women*), Kraft, Lexus, Merrill Lynch, NetJets, Oakley, Rolex.

FIGURE 8.13

It is always important to present a consistent brand image, especially from a visual perspective. Use pictures that are already approved and which are consistent with a celebrity's personality.

Used with permission.

PERSONAL BRANDS

- Every individual has a personal brand identity whether he or she likes it or not.
- All people can decide whether they want to turn up their brand's volume or mute it.
- Personal brand principles include:
  - Understand and care about how others perceive me.
  - Adopt a promise related to how I want other people to feel.
  - Act and behave in a manner that benefits and affirms others.
- When describing a personal promise, it's important to answer these questions:
  - How do I want other people to describe me?
  - What is my most distinctive attribute?
  - How will I enhance other people's lives?
- Being a real professional in any field is more than an extensive education or specific expertise. It's about being perceived as a professional related to one's actions and behaviors.
- For celebrities of all types, it is important to develop a plan for their brand success and not become a victim of success.

CHAPTER

Specialized BrandPromise Applications

Focus on enhancing your members' and clients' success!

This chapter focuses on specialized BrandPromise applications for:

1. Member-centric businesses
2. Charitable and philanthropic organizations
3. Professional services
4. Associations

It includes brand profiles for SAFE Credit Union, Make-A-Wish Foundation, Callison Architecture, and the Destination Marketing Association International.

As the world of "branding" has evolved, the science has moved beyond the traditional focus on consumer packaged goods to embrace a wide range of broader applications.

One of the most appealing methodologies associated with the study of BrandScience is the understanding that "perception is reality." In other words, regardless of how intelligent an organization's strategic plan is, if the target audience does not internalize the desired perception, nothing else matters.

Hence, every kind of organization imaginable including charitable, philanthropic, nonprofit, member-centric, and even

FIGURE 9.1

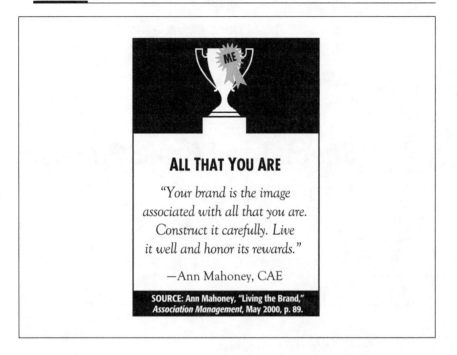

ALL THAT YOU ARE

*"Your brand is the image
associated with all that you are.
Construct it carefully. Live
it well and honor its rewards."*

—Ann Mahoney, CAE

**SOURCE: Ann Mahoney, "Living the Brand,"
Association Management, May 2000, p. 89.**

professional service firms such as lawyers, doctors, and dentists
are interested in enhancing their respective brand's perception.
Organizations that ignore the principles of BrandScience today
are charting a course for competitive disadvantage and an
increased chance of failure.

This chapter focuses on four specialized types of organizations that have applied the BrandPromise principles to enhance
their success. These roadmaps for brand success include member-
centric businesses such as credit unions and co-ops, charitable
and philanthropic organizations and foundations, professional
service firms, and associations and societies.

The necessary mindset and process for these specialized
organizations is the same as we outlined in Chapters 1 to 3, and
especially in the Destination BrandScience chapter (Chapter 7).
However, achieving a promise commitment across all stakeholders for specialized types of organizations can be much more
tedious and time consuming. Unlike a corporation which may

mandate a new brand direction, associations or member-centric organizations must gain a large consensus among their members in order to achieve a significant strategic change.

1. MEMBER-CENTRIC BUSINESSES

Member-centric businesses include a wide variety of organizations such as co-ops, credit unions, and country clubs. In fact, they could include any institution that focuses on benefits for its members. For the purposes of our discussion here, we focus on credit unions as a representative example of a member-centric business.

First, a few thoughts about member-centric service. I was always under the impression that member-centric businesses provide exemplary service. However, based on a significant amount of research, it would appear that there is room for improvement in member-centric brands. It is my belief that many member-centric businesses could significantly enhance the perceived value to their members if they were to adopt the promise mindset and make a promise to their members that's related to exceptional experiences.

Typically, most member-centric businesses have missions, visions, or values, or a combination of these. An examination reveals that many lack a commitment to an exceptional member experience. Here are a few typical statements from member-centric organizations:

- Support the economic welfare of our members
- Lowest cost through group purchases
- Highest-quality products and services
- Support a low-impact, nonharmful approach to the environment

Every member-centric business should make the commitment to provide exceptional member experiences. At the end of the day, it's all about the experience. Everyone wants to be greeted by happy, proactive, energetic associates who are well trained, act like professionals, and make their members feel great.

A brand's relationship with members should begin with a dialogue, and that conversation should continue throughout the relationship. Too often when someone becomes a member of an insurance company plan or other type of organization, the "dialogue mentality" disappears after the initial buy-in because the organization thinks that it knows what's best for the member.

Figure 9.2 illustrates the importance of an ongoing dialogue with members, frontline employees, and executives and managers.

Eric Heia, an executive with a large regional insurance carrier, explains that a member-centric relationship "requires a three-dimensional permanent dialogue that includes members and the organization's leadership as well as the frontline associate's point of view. It is essential to have the associate's input because they deal with the members every day and understand how they feel."

FIGURE 9.2

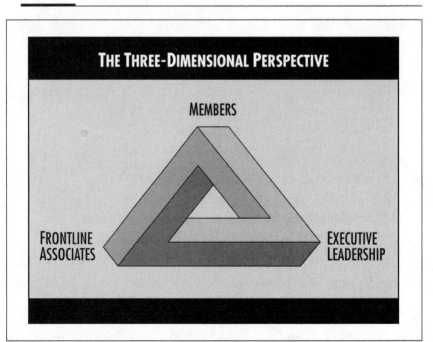

Why not include selected frontline associates to participate in every major discussion that relates to a policy or procedure change that will affect a member's experience?

Many credit unions have been quick to realize the benefits of building a genuine brand and making a real promise to their members. Prime examples include Affinity Federal Credit Union of New Jersey and Washington State Employees Credit Union.

The question to ask any member-centric organization is: Are we creating "passionate advocates"? The SAFE Credit Union profile provides excellent insight into how to move beyond "satisfaction sameness" and to make a promise and become a genuine brand.

BRAND PROFILE

SAFE CREDIT UNION

SAFE Credit Union is a nonprofit financial institution serving the Sacramento metropolitan area. There are over 60 financial institutions serving the Sacramento area, and SAFE is the seventh-largest financial institution in the Sacramento region. SAFE Credit Union needed a way to differentiate itself from the many other financial institutions around Sacramento. The best way to do that was to create a promise and a member experience that would deliver the desired perception in its members' minds.

The development of SAFE's promise, as indicated in Figure 9.4, was the result of its annual board and senior management retreat. A brand team was organized with selected executives and board members who were assigned the task of developing the promise. The members of the team completed an assessment of their brand utilizing member research and one-on-one interviews with key influencers. As a result of this yearlong effort, the brand team recommended a promise. SAFE's brand promise is to provide members with exceptional experiences, best solutions, and professional experts to help them enjoy life. SAFE realized that by helping members improve their financial well-being, it could also help them *enjoy life*.

After the promise was created, it became clear that without a real organizational transformation, the promise would not

FIGURE 9.3

Used with permission.

FIGURE 9.4

achieve SAFE's expectations. Executive management and the board agreed to begin a process of transformation that would create a unique member experience in order to distinguish their credit union as a true brand. Even though SAFE already enjoyed high levels of member satisfaction, it conducted monthly mystery shops to measure service levels at its branches and the branches of the five competitive financial institutions with the largest market share in the area. "Mystery shops" involve unannounced service evaluations by customer service professionals who act as though they are customers. While SAFE received the highest ratings by the independent research firm that conducted the mystery shop research, very satisfied members were not enough. SAFE wanted members to be passionate advocates for its brand.

SAFE came to the conclusion that its members really had only two needs: put money in and take money out. All too often financial institutions complicate the process by dividing the business into departments or "silos," such as deposits, auto loans, mortgage loans, and branches.

FIGURE 9.5

SAFE's promise was intended to remind everyone that the only reason to put money in and take money out is for members to "enjoy their lives."

It began the transformation by focusing on how to encourage associate behaviors that create exceptional member experiences. It believed that the best way to change associate behavior was to address three areas: associate performance evaluations, associate training, and associate awards. Performance evaluations, training, and award criteria needed to be based on behaviors that would create exceptional member experiences. The following conclusions became apparent:

- Associate behavior is strongly influenced by training.
- Associates are focused on how to improve their performance evaluation ratings.
- Associates are motivated to qualify for company awards and therefore will be likely to adopt the behaviors needed to qualify them for awards and improved performance evaluations.

SAFE's board of directors actively participated in the process. The changes to the performance evaluation process, associate training, and associate awards criteria were just the start. Work teams met and discussed their promise and how they would make it a part of their everyday routine.

One of the first positive developments was a member welcome program. New members were called within three days after their account was opened and given a personal welcome. The representative also asked if the account-opening process was a good experience for the new member. The caller offered to follow up if there were any unresolved issues. If applicable, the caller then confirmed the date and amount of the first loan payment for the member. Members appreciated that SAFE was helping them make sure their loan payment was set on the date they requested and that the payment was what they had agreed to at the time of the loan. Before finishing the conversation, the representative then offered members other preapproved loan offers such as the opportunity to refinance an existing loan from another financial institution with SAFE at a lower monthly payment without an extension of the term or at other favorable terms. Members commented that they were impressed that the credit union was able to immediately help them begin saving money in a way that was consistent with the goal of improving their financial well-being. Over 25 percent of these calls resulted in the credit union being able to meet an additional financial need for their members. This further enhances the delivery of its promise.

With lots of competitive choices for members, it's important that its promise is kept. Henry Wirz, president and chief executive officer of SAFE, points out that what matters the most is whether your members are "passionate advocates" for your brand. Each personal story he hears from his members reinforces the brand success.

This "passionate advocate" concept is consistent with a very popular management science concept known as "net promoter." Its supporters believe that the *net promoter* concept is a great way to measure customer attitudes toward an organization. It is based on a single question: How likely is it that you would recommend us to a friend or colleague?

Henry feels that SAFE's promise is making a real difference. He recently attended a board meeting for another organization, and one of the board members told him how much she enjoyed being a member of SAFE. She indicated that at her branch the associates know her and that she often waits for her favorite associate so that she can visit with her "friend" and transact her business. This is the type of exceptional service that leads to a significant number of new member accounts from referrals. The best compliment is a referral from existing members because it confirms that the promise is distinguishing the perception of the credit union. SAFE's BrandPromise is flourishing, and more members are becoming passionate advocates.

SAFE's desire to create *passionate advocates* takes the genuine brand philosophy to the next level. Customer service as a concept has become meaningless in many cases because it doesn't specify how you want your members (customers) to feel. Passionate advocates instill a proactive desire to delight members in a way that energizes and enhances a brand.

2. CHARITABLE AND PHILANTHROPIC ORGANIZATIONS

Nonprofit organizations are one of the largest market segments existing today. Expenditures by nonprofit groups totaled almost $945 billion and accounted for about 9% of the gross domestic product of the United States in 2003, according to the National Council of Nonprofit Associations.[1]

Mary Lower, the chief storyteller for the Sterling Cross Communications Group, explains, "Nonprofit organizations are probably best known by the services they provide to people in need. But it is important to remember that charitable organizations also create the space and opportunity for individuals to engage in volunteerism and become actively involved in civic life. By connecting people, inspiring altruism, and giving voice to local and far-reaching concerns, nonprofits weave an uninterrupted web of connection that binds communities together."[2]

A strong economy and successful firms like Microsoft, with its large associate equity base, have created enormous wealth. This has contributed to significant growth in foundations and billions of dollars of contributions.

Charitable organizations are different from traditional corporate organizations in several important ways:

1. They tend to be more consensus-oriented in their decision-making process.
2. Charitable organizations usually involve volunteers, and they can be challenging to manage and slow to embrace change.
3. Nonprofits usually have limited executive and support personnel to develop and implement new strategies.
4. There is a misperception among many nonprofit organizations that the brand is the logo, typeface, or graphics.
5. People associated with charitable or philanthropic organizations are very passionate about their cause and usually consider their work to be a personal mission.

"It is essential for a nonprofit to have a 15-second 'elevator' pitch that clearly explains what they do," according to Dirk Rinker, president of Campbell Rinker, one of the leading marketing research firms for the nonprofit industry. He adds, "The promise must be easily understood, otherwise it will be difficult to compete with other organizations for donor's attention and financial support."

It is also important for nonprofits to embrace the concept of consistent communications with their volunteers, donors, and influencers. They are all looking for cues to reinforce a nonprofit's integrity and trustworthiness.

Rinker explains that to live up to donor service quality expectations, a nonprofit's communication's strategy should constantly reinforce that it is:

- Doing good work and creating positive real outcomes
- Financially accountable and fiscally responsible
- Professionally managed

In the for-profit world, brands generally represent tangible products and services; there is an exchange of value that happens at the time of purchase. In the nonprofit arena, the exchange of value centers around "good feelings" or more of an intangible deliverable for those who contribute, support, and volunteer. This makes it all the more important that a nonprofit develop and live the right promise.

The benefits of the right promise are many. According to a *Marketing News* article, "With a concerted effort and investment of time, nonprofit organizations can generate significantly more of what matters, including:

- Increased profile and visibility
- Ability to attract and retain loyal members, clients, donors, volunteers and program participants
- Increased credibility and legitimacy
- Differentiation in a crowded nonprofit marketplace
- Ability to make and sustain long-term relationships
- Most importantly, increased revenue"[3]

The following brand profile of the Make-A-Wish Foundation provides strategic insights on how to make a promise and deliver a nonprofit brand successfully.

BRAND PROFILE

MAKE-A-WISH FOUNDATION

THE TRUE BRAND

The Make-A-Wish Foundation grants the wishes of children with life-threatening medical conditions to enrich the human experience with hope, strength, and joy. Created in 1980 when a group of caring individuals helped a young boy fulfill his dream of

FIGURE 9.6

Used with permission.

becoming a police officer, the foundation is now the largest wish-
granting charity in the world, with 69 chapters in the United
States and its territories. With the help of generous donors and
nearly 25,000 volunteers, the Make-A-Wish Foundation grants
more than 12,600 wishes a year and has granted more than
150,000 wishes in the United States since its inception.

The Make-A-Wish name is a true brand because it is
focused, strong, trusted, and consistent in the delivery of its
promise. Moreover, it strikes a positive emotional cord in the
public consciousness. "The clarity and laser focus of our mission
is one of the driving forces behind the strength of our brand,"
says David Williams, president and chief executive officer of the
Make-A-Wish Foundation of America.

Make-A-Wish focuses on one thing—grant wishes—and
they constantly challenge themselves to do it beyond the wildest
expectations of the children they serve. Their recipients tran-
scend every socioeconomic status, race, religion and political
belief because the medical conditions they are dealing with can
affect anyone. This helps give the Make-A-Wish Foundation
broad appeal, free of some of the barriers and biases that other
not-for-profit organizations may face. David explains, "Our work
taps the public's emotions in powerful ways. Deep down inside,
we can all remember the excitement we felt when pursuing our
childhood wishes. And when we get to experience a wish firsthand, it creates an emotional resonance that transports us to
that feeling of carefree joy we felt in our childhood."

Although the foundation has evolved over time from a group
of loosely organized volunteers to establishing performance
standards that ensure that every wish granted is magical and

the best that it can be, its mission has not wavered. It remains true to its brand promise of granting the most heartfelt wishes to these kids at a time when they need it most.

For many of the same reasons that the public is fond of the Make-A-Wish Foundation, the media also pay it quite a bit of attention. The foundation is featured in more than 400 news stories a month in the United States. This equates to more than 1 billion media impressions annually. The foundation works diligently to coordinate and manage these opportunities and correct the occasional misperception that all wish kids are terminally ill.

With a wish being granted somewhere in the United States every 41 minutes, the opportunity for confusing messages is significant. In response to this issue, the foundation has developed numerous communications and brand standards and resources that are available to its chapters and corporate partners via the Internet. The ease of use, strength, and consistency of these resources further helps to minimize inaccurate representations.

FIGURE 9.7

Reprinted with permission.

After existing for its first 20 years under the banner of its original wishbone logo, the foundation decided to improve its graphic identity. With the help of some leading brand developers and a lot of research, it devised a new logo featuring the Make-A-Wish name and a star-and-swirl icon. The logo has global appeal, is free of cultural taboos associated with bones, and captures the magic and whimsy of what the brand has become.

In its 25th year, the foundation chose to go deeper than the logo and worked to clarify its brand attributes, including its personality, character, and tone. According to Mike Pressendo, director of brand communications for the Make-A-Wish Foundation of America, "There are many fantastic children's charities doing admirable work throughout the world every day. In order to grow our brand in that environment, we needed to stand apart from the others. We needed to differentiate and make it easier for the public to recognize the Make-A-Wish Foundation in a crowded field of nonprofits."

The foundation began by analyzing how the other children's charities were positioning their brands. That research found that once you took away the logos from their brand vehicles, most became indistinguishable from each other. Then the research homed in on what the Make-A-Wish Foundation could uniquely own in the minds of the public while ringing true to its volunteers, supporters, and staff. Once those attributes were agreed on, they were communicated to Make-A-Wish associates and volunteers in an easy-to-understand brand standards guide. Then the foundation became zealous in reinforcing these attributes.

Subsequently, the foundation revamped all its brand vehicles (Web site, collateral, advertisements, and even its work environment) to align design, images, and tone of all communications with the new standards. "We knew it had really become part of our organizational DNA when people at all levels, from accounting to IT, began espousing and promoting our unique brand attributes," Pressendo said.

FOCUS ON THE JOY

It is an inescapable fact that all the children the foundation serves are dealing with life-threatening conditions. However, the Make-A-Wish Foundation is not involved in the medical

FIGURE 9.8

Good Housekeeping® magazine rated the
Make-A-Wish Foundation as one of the "best
charities for kids," and SELF editors selected the
foundation to the magazine's "recommended"
list in its Charity Giving Guide.

The Make-A-Wish Foundation is one of only three
nonprofits honored as one of America's greatest
brands in America's Greatest Brands,
Volume Three.

The Make-A-Wish Foundation also consistently
ranks among the nation's top 100 charities in
publications such as Forbes and nonprofit trades,
The Chronicle of Philanthropy and
The NonProfit Times.

Used with permission.

aspect of helping these kids feel better. Instead, it provides joy-ful experiences for these kids and their families that give them control of something in their life at a time when everything seems out of control. Also, it gives them something to look for-ward to. They can wish for nearly anything, and the foundation's volunteers, staff, and supporters will move mountains to deliver on these wishes. Moreover, the wish experience tends to provide respite and escape from the medical regimens the children often must endure. A wish experience has the power not just to put a smile on a kid's face, but to be a bright spot in the lives of every-one involved—families, donors, volunteers, sponsors, and even communities.

The foundation could have taken the path of positioning its brand around the difficult circumstances its wish kids face and could have sought to generate support through public sympathy and pity. However, that would have been out of sync with what the brand had already become on its own. Although the Make-A-Wish brand attributes are multifaceted, the essence of the brand can be distilled to a single word—*joy*. It was not so much that it decided to be that way. Instead, it was recognized that joy permeates all aspects of how the foundation fulfills its brand promise—its mission.

Every wish the foundation grants is a powerful story capa-ble of tapping the emotions of all who encounter it, whether an active participant or a casual observer. These positive emotions can make for positive associations. Marketers have recognized the influence this can have on purchase behavior, which has led to the rising popularity of cause marketing. More and more, con-sumers want to make a difference with their purchases.

Another important brand asset that is critical to the strength of the Make-A-Wish brand, or any other brand for that matter, is trust. Therefore, the foundation is very careful to

FIGURE 9.9

ensure that the brands it aligns with through corporate sponsor-ships and cause marketing initiatives are compatible with its brand and have admirable reputations.

Today, a visit to a Make-A-Wish office can be a joyful expe-rience in and of itself. You will find its work environments adorned with joyful images of kids delighting in their most heartfelt wishes. The joy is reflected in the writing style of its communications, from brochures and newsletters to Web sites and associate orientation materials. Even its meetings and work groups have a joyful air. It is truly an inspiring organiza-tion and epitomizes a true brand where associates and volun-teers all share a passion and commitment to bringing the promise to life: magical, joy-filled wishes to Make-A-Wish kids everywhere.

3. PROFESSIONAL SERVICE FIRMS

It can be a difficult challenge to achieve a brand mindset within a professional service firm. Many professionals seem to believe that if they are really good at what they do, such as being a smart doctor, attorney, or engineer, then that's the most impor-tant measure.

It's essential to have the appropriate professional expertise as the foundation for building a professional service brand. However, in today's world, that's not enough to reach genuine brand status. It requires a keen understanding of what level of emotional connection you desire to make with clients. A firm may provide good advice, but if the billing department and invoicing procedures frustrate clients, then it will be difficult, if not impossible, to create the preferred image, perception, and the loyalty that is desired.

As an example, a professional service firm's telephone sys-tem may be a key determinant of its client's emotional equity in the firm. A live operator or a live answering service that's seem-less to clients may be the first place to begin. It also can enhance clients' perceptions related to a firm's success, capability, and expertise. According to Eric Siegel, a lecturer in management at the Goergen Entrepreneurial Management Program, "Perception in the marketplace is a significant factor to success."[4]

As was discussed in Chapter 3, the balance between functional and emotional attributes is extremely important. Professional service firms seem to focus on the functional side of the relationship with their clients. This preoccupation with functional activities can be a disadvantage to a professional service firm because of the perceptions created in the minds of its clients. Whenever I hear people say they are unhappy with their doctor, lawyer, Realtor, or whatever, they always complain about the way the professional made them feel. Clients usually become dissatisfied because the professional wasn't responsive in a timely manner, didn't look out for their best interests, or just didn't seem to care.

A study reported in the *Mayo Clinic Proceedings Journal* "found that when patients were asked to describe their best and worst experiences with doctors, technical expertise was rarely mentioned. Instead, the best doctors were described as honest, compassionate, respectful and thorough; the worst were arrogant, callous and dismissive."[5]

"Any individual business, especially one that provides professional services, that doesn't subscribe to the BrandPromise philosophy is missing out on a key ingredient necessary to attract and maintain loyal customers today." Mike Webber should know. In the film and video production business he participates on both sides of the equation, as vice president of MainSail Productions, a video production company, and as president of Nightfly Entertainment.

"The principles related to thinking like a genuine brand have changed the way I view the consumer/company relationship and also changed the way I do business," says Webber.

The opportunity for professional service firms to improve their emotional connections with their clients is significant, and that begins with making a promise. The Callison brand profile outlines the right kind of mindset needed to become a genuine brand.

BRAND PROFILE

CALLISON ARCHITECTURE

Born and raised in Seattle, entrepreneur Anthony Callison opened his first office soon after graduating from the University of Washington in 1960. As an architect and businessperson, he concentrated on building his firm through strong interpersonal relationships and project diversity. By 1975, his small architectural firm had expanded into the Callison Partnership as it forged its first links with Nordstrom, a family-owned fashion specialty store which was just beginning the growth and expansion that has turned it into a retail legend. Although Tony Callison died unexpectedly in 1988, he provided the spirit for his small firm to turn into one of the most successful architectural practices in the world.

Callison has enjoyed a very positive reputation and relationship with its clients, and like most successful professional service firms, it has focused on providing the best expertise for its clients.

Several years ago, the firm began a review of its professional practice as part of a long-term strategic plan. Its Brand Assessment revealed an opportunity to distinguish its brand. Successful architectural firms were expected to provide excellent design. However, the research indicated that the opportunity to become a one-of-a-kind brand would be related to its ability to positively affect its clients' business.

Callison's leadership was ahead of its time in recognizing the opportunity to begin to think like a genuine brand. It became focused on the "user" or customer of each newly designed retail environment, hotel, or mixed-use project. Combining this perspective with its clients' desires created an

FIGURE 9.10

Used with permission.

"experience" mindset within the firm. This "experience" focus provided the foundation for its promise.

Bill Karst, chief executive officer of Callison explains, "What differentiates us from other firms is our approach in creating a distinctive sense of place by aligning our clients' business objectives with their brand identity and vision to create the right experience."

The Callison promise is reflected in the company's commitment to create value for its clients by envisioning design as a business strategy and not just for the sake of design.

According to Karst, "Our user-driven approach is to design environments for the people that will actually experience our work whether they are customers, residents, guests, employees, or patients in order to generate strategic returns for our clients and emotional returns for communities."

FIGURE 9.11

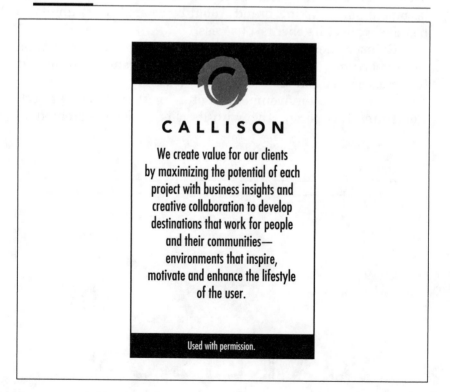

CALLISON

We create value for our clients by maximizing the potential of each project with business insights and creative collaboration to develop destinations that work for people and their communities— environments that inspire, motivate and enhance the lifestyle of the user.

Used with permission.

Recognizing the emotional impact of a well-designed building, or for that matter any environment, is the right thought process for a professional service firm to become a genuine brand. Too often, professional service firms fall into the trap of believing that quality expertise is enough to be successful. Expertise is obviously required of any professional, but it is a professional's understanding of how to deliver the right emotional experience that distinguishes genuine brands.

Awards are an important part of all professional fields. However, the award that counts the most is the one that's reflected in the emotional satisfaction in the mind of the end user. Callison's dedication to inspire, motivate, and enhance the lifestyle of the people who experience its architectural design is the kind of paradigm shift that takes a professional service firm to the next level.

Callison's promise and its philosophy have earned it the rewards of being a genuine brand. Growing from 10 employees in 1975 to 700 in 2007, the company has been honored with enough awards, designations, and accolades to fill a trophy room. It has been ranked the number-one retail design firm in the world for the last five years, beginning with 2002, and has received many other top rankings in various design categories from *Interior Design Magazine, Retail Design, Building Design and Construction,* and many others. Callison has something to be truly proud of by contributing more than $1 million annually to its community.

4. ASSOCIATION BRANDSCIENCE

In the past, you would not necessarily look to associations to discover the best-demonstrated brand practices. In fact, most associations were guided by mission statements that generally focused on various services for their members. Associations communicated with their members about products, services, and meetings rather than image, perception, and a universal promise.

However, all that has changed. In fact, many professional associations have been setting new standards for the practice of BrandScience because their members want to be perceived as more relevant and more valued in their respective fields.

I recall a presentation to a state association of eye doctors over 10 years ago. The presentation pointed out the imminent brand challenge by retail optical brands such as LensCrafters and the like. The leadership of the association summarily dismissed the need for a brand perspective much less a promise with the statement, "We don't sell toothpaste." However, within a couple of years, we began advising several medical associations in their pursuit of successful strategies for their brand and a promise for their members. A decade ago, it used to be enough for an association to have a good annual meeting and provide an opportunity for member networking and education. However, in the association world, as well as all member-focused environments, things have changed dramatically.

During our early work with the American Society of Association Executives, we discovered a revolutionary paradigm shift. Previously, it was widely held that if a member-based organization focused on its relationship with its members, everything would be fine. In fact, I can remember some association executives saying, "Our members' relationship with their clients, patients, or customers is not our business."

The paradigm shift we discovered was that a professional association's relationships with its members would be directly linked to the quality of its members' relationships with their respective clients, patients, or customers. In addition, the clients', patients', or customers' perceptions of an association's professional members, such as lawyers or doctors, would determine its members' ultimate respect, recognition, and business success. Why? Because the public's perception and trust in many professionals has been declining. Hence, members of professional organizations began to demand that their associations improve their public's perceptions including recognition, respect, value, and relevance.

It's essential for associations and societies to create strategies for their brand with two perspectives in mind:

1. *External:* The relevant marketplace (industry) in which an association's or society's members conduct business.

2. *Internal:* The organization's brand.

A successful association or society brand initiative should always begin with a focus on enhancing their members' perception, image, and success; that is, the external brand. Once that strategy has been outlined, then the organization can address its internal brand, as illustrated in Figure 9.12, and how that should align with its members' goals.

As an example, the American Medical Association recently began an advertising campaign focused on providing examples of how doctors have improved specific patients' lives. This campaign recognizes the importance and value of a positive external public perception of its members. It also signals a change in association priorities, and associations are now recognizing the fundamental importance of a promise approach and their public's perception of their professional members.

FIGURE 9.12

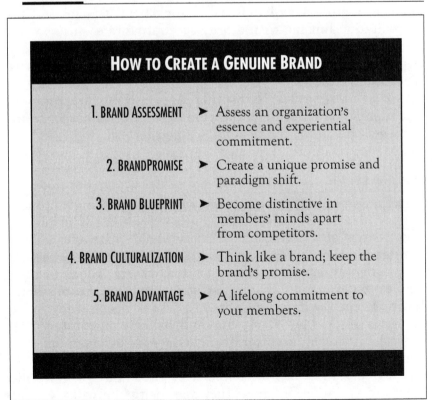

HOW TO CREATE A GENUINE BRAND

1. BRAND ASSESSMENT	➤ Assess an organization's essence and experiential commitment.
2. BRANDPROMISE	➤ Create a unique promise and paradigm shift.
3. BRAND BLUEPRINT	➤ Become distinctive in members' minds apart from competitors.
4. BRAND CULTURALIZATION	➤ Think like a brand; keep the brand's promise.
5. BRAND ADVANTAGE	➤ A lifelong commitment to your members.

In some cases, associations have been too quick to jump on the internal "branding" bandwagon and have focused first on the association brand or logo. It is extremely important that any association or society brand initiative follow the process outlined in Chapter 1 and that the analysis begin from the members' perspective. The members are the first priority for an association's brand work and the members', clients', or customers' perspectives complete the process. In other words, a change in an association's brand identity needs must be relevant for both the members and their customers or clients.

An excellent example is the Heart Rhythm Society (formerly the North American Society of Pacing and Electrophysiology). The Heart Rhythm Society's brand initiative followed a comprehensive process. It was not just a "new logo" exercise.

Leading associations and societies are also learning that a new brand initiative needs to be in lockstep with a formal member accreditation program that ensures that their members are following a professional approach in their field of expertise. This accreditation linkage with a brand initiative raises the bar for professional development and industry standards that are essential in today's quickly changing marketplace to reinforce trust and integrity.

The Destination Marketing Association International brand profile outlines the best-demonstrated practices for creating a genuine brand for associations and societies.

BRAND PROFILE

DESTINATION MARKETING ASSOCIATION INTERNATIONAL

The boards of International Association of Convention and Visitors Bureaus (now known as the Destination Marketing Association International) and its foundation rolled up their sleeves to develop a long-term strategy for their organization's future. Primed with the insights of a future trends study, member focus group results, and hundreds of influencer interviews, they identified the need for an industrywide strategy for their members' brands as one of four key issues for their success.

The organization was founded in 1914 and is the world's largest association of convention and visitor bureaus (CVBs),

FIGURE 9.13

Used with permission.

serving more than 1,600 members in over 650 destination marketing organizations in over 33 countries.

Convention and visitor bureaus and tourism boards were being challenged by a host of aggressive travel and tourism intermediaries; not to mention significant changes in the way business was being conducted as a result of new technology.

In response to its members desire to improve its competitive advantage, distinctive perception, image, and level of success, the organization launched its brand leadership campaign, which is a comprehensive project to create a long-term strategy relating to all aspects of the association's and its members' brand success. Figure 9.14 illustrates the project phases associated with the brand leadership campaign.

In addition to the steps outlined in Figure 9.14, the project included an evaluation of the association's brand identity as well as the development of a destination BrandScience book that would guide members in their development of their individual destination brands.

The internal communications began with the production of a video titled "The Power of Branding" for all members to use. This fast-paced video was designed like a movie promotional trailer to excite the members about the advantages of applying the BrandScience methodology to destinations.

The Brand Assessment provided the basis for a consensus for future direction. As Michael Gehrisch, president and chief executive officer of the Destination Marketing Association International, relates, "We have a real responsibility to ensure

FIGURE 9.14

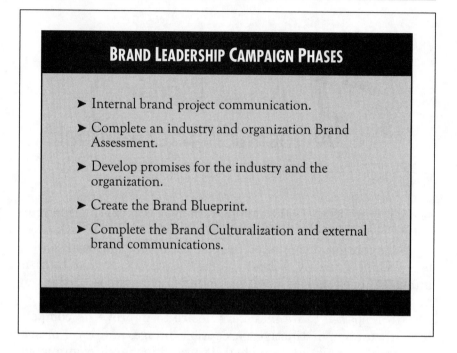

BRAND LEADERSHIP CAMPAIGN PHASES

➤ Internal brand project communication.

➤ Complete an industry and organization Brand Assessment.

➤ Develop promises for the industry and the organization.

➤ Create the Brand Blueprint.

➤ Complete the Brand Culturalization and external brand communications.

our relevance, distinction, and position in the marketplace to optimize our member's success in every community."

The brand leadership project provided the basis for a focus across the industry on the future success factors for destination brands, that is, the association's members. The association's promise was the result of a realization that the industry really should focus on the "destination experience." The external promise that was developed for their members is reflected in Figure 9.15.

The association's existing identity was also assessed and evaluated. It became clear that a change from the Convention & Visitors Bureau identity to a destination mindset was the best-demonstrated practice for the future and the right driver for the future Brand Blueprint as indicated in Figure 9.16.

The members overwhelmingly approved the new image and brand identity in 2006, and a new chapter began for the destination industry.

The brand leadership campaign was vigorously supported by the association's members and led by Reint Reinders, who

FIGURE 9.15

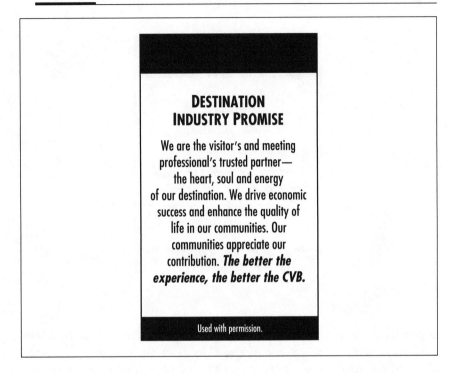

DESTINATION INDUSTRY PROMISE

We are the visitor's and meeting professional's trusted partner— the heart, soul and energy of our destination. We drive economic success and enhance the quality of life in our communities. Our communities appreciate our contribution. *The better the experience, the better the CVB.*

Used with permission.

FIGURE 9.16

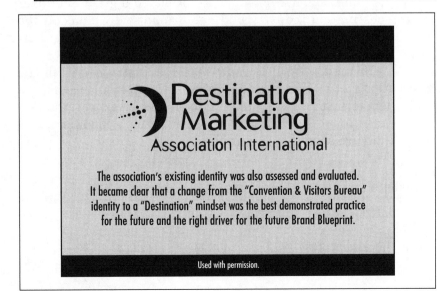

The association's existing identity was also assessed and evaluated. It became clear that a change from the "Convention & Visitors Bureau" identity to a "Destination" mindset was the best demonstrated practice for the future and the right driver for the future Brand Blueprint.

Used with permission.

FIGURE 9.17

PROMISE TO OUR MEMBERS

We are the most reliable and knowledgeable resource for official destination marketing organizations. *Your success is our success.*

Used with permission.

was the secretary/treasurer of the association and the president and chief executive officer of the San Diego CVB. He concluded that, "The importance of making the right promise and keeping it can not be overstated."

The brand leadership campaign provided a great energizer for the destination industry and has dramatically changed the way destinations conduct their business and think about their responsibility for the visitor's experience.

The Brand Culturalization phase was instrumental in the association's executive team examining its internal promise to their members. It was concluded that the association staff members should make a promise to the association's members, and the results are shown in Figure 9.17.

THOUGHT GUIDE

SPECIALIZED BRANDPROMISE APPLICATIONS

- The BrandPromise methodology applies to any type of organization including member-centric businesses, charitable and philanthropic organizations, professional services, associations.

- Regardless of how intelligent an organization's strategy plan is, if the target audience does not internalize the desired perception, nothing else matters.
- Member-centric businesses should deliver exceptional experiences.
- A brand's relationship with its members should begin with a dialogue that continues throughout the relationship.
- In the for-profit world, brands generally market tangible products and services. In the nonprofit arena, the exchange centers around "good feelings" or more of an intangible for those who contribute, support, and volunteer. This makes it all the more important that a nonprofit develop and live the right promise.
- It is essential that professional service firms be really good at what they do; however, genuine professional service brands are built by making strong emotional connections with clients.
- An association's ultimate success will be closely related to its members' promise to their customers, clients, patients, and so on.
- Association brand initiatives should be closely linked to standards and member accreditation.

CHAPTER 10

Promise Perspectives

The Detailed Process for Building Genuine Brands

Another person's point of view is an opportunity to improve your own perspective.

CONCLUSION

In the previous chapters we provided the methodology to follow for creating promises that build genuine brands regardless of the type, size, or business of an organization. This chapter provides a variety of perspectives to enhance the process of developing promises.

One question must be constantly asked and answered by each and every person associated with a brand: What's our promise, and how do I deliver it? In order to address this question, the following conditions must be present in an organization:

1. The organization must embrace a customer-centric philosophy.
2. A proven scientific methodology must be utilized to develop an effective promise.
3. Every person associated with the organization needs to be passionate about delivering the promise.

THE GENUINE BRAND PROCESS

The following pages outline the genuine brand process which was first introduced in our book *BrandMindset*. The process has evolved over time, and this represents our latest thinking.

A genuine brand should inspire people to aspire, and it should invoke a positive feeling as well as a sense of pride. The genuine brand process should be focused on identifying, communicating, and delivering a brand's distinctive characteristics, those that are important and beneficial to its stakeholders and especially to its customers and prospective customers.

Being Distinctive Is Not Optional

Genuine brands rise above in the marketplace and are sought by consumers because of their distinctive qualities and attributes.

FIGURE 10.1

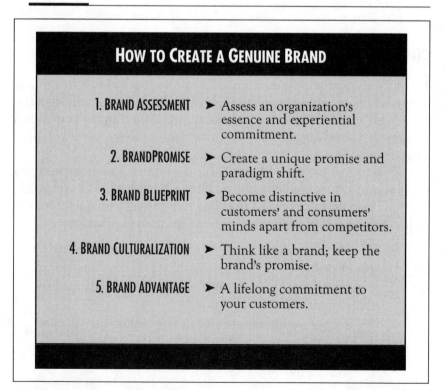

HOW TO CREATE A GENUINE BRAND	
1. BRAND ASSESSMENT	➤ Assess an organization's essence and experiential commitment.
2. BRANDPROMISE	➤ Create a unique promise and paradigm shift.
3. BRAND BLUEPRINT	➤ Become distinctive in customers' and consumers' minds apart from competitors.
4. BRAND CULTURALIZATION	➤ Think like a brand; keep the brand's promise.
5. BRAND ADVANTAGE	➤ A lifelong commitment to your customers.

Understanding and applying the concept of distinction is not an option when it comes to creating genuine brands. It is a *requirement*.

Building brands is tough enough in a rapidly changing marketplace. It takes a period of time to become established in the minds of customers. While the timing may vary by industry and by the size or type of organization, all face similar challenges related to gaining brand recognition, competitive advantage, product and service life cycles, production, development, lead times, and delivery to market.

Brand extensions often do not work because they are not perceived as distinctive by consumers or are inconsistent with how a brand is perceived. They only work when the concept is unique and provides a compelling reason for the customer to buy. Supermarket shelves are filled with hundreds of brand extensions up and down every aisle. Many are failures because they are simply another me-too product. The only people who think they are *different* are the manufacturers who created them. The primary reason organizations develop brand extensions seems to be for growth or to retain "share of shelf" in order to protect or grow market share. In reality, the best way to protect and increase market share is by creating brands consumers perceive as *distinctive*—that possess some or all of the key attributes discussed earlier.

The discovery of powerful distinctive attributes occurs during the Brand Assessment phase of the doctrine process. If a brand is to be distinctive, there are endless possibilities and countless options that can be explored. The secret is to select or develop distinctive attributes that customers and prospective customers will value the most and seek out the brand for.

The Brand Assessment

Brand Assessment is about objectivity. The process is designed to characterize current perceptions based on factual information and data as well as observable conclusions in a manner that rules out or confirms subjective influences (gut feelings, intuition, opinions, etc.). Think of it as an audit that is required to verify the condition of the organization's brand image, position, and perception.

FIGURE 10.2

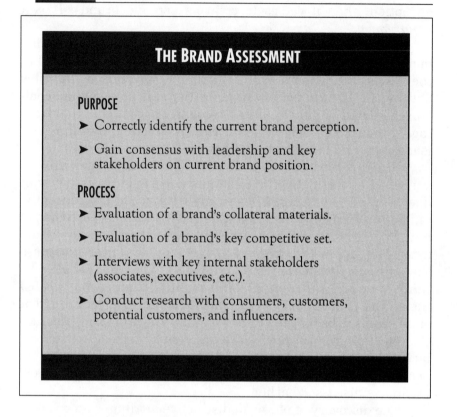

THE BRAND ASSESSMENT

PURPOSE

➤ Correctly identify the current brand perception.

➤ Gain consensus with leadership and key stakeholders on current brand position.

PROCESS

➤ Evaluation of a brand's collateral materials.

➤ Evaluation of a brand's key competitive set.

➤ Interviews with key internal stakeholders (associates, executives, etc.).

➤ Conduct research with consumers, customers, potential customers, and influencers.

The assessment helps the brand determine "where it is" in the minds of customers, potential customers, and all stakeholders. It's difficult to plan a future strategy if the organization doesn't know where the brand is perceived today. The brand can't move forward or achieve its goal to be a genuine brand without a thorough understanding of customers (obtained through research), the business environment, its marketing strategy (what's worked, what hasn't, and why or why not), customer behavior (transaction analysis), market and competitive trends, consumer trends, and technology migration and application, among others.

Once all the research has been completed and information gathered, a written report on each should be prepared following a common outline:

- Background (purpose, methodology, sources, etc.)
- Brand conclusions (each one supported by fact or reference)
- Brand recommendations
- Quotes to consider (stakeholder quotes noted during research or brand-related quotes that are relevant)
- Exhibits (copies of reports, research findings, sources, and articles to support conclusions)

Typically, an overall executive summary is written based on the assessment research and is distributed to executives in order to achieve a consensus on how the brand is perceived and what attributes are desired by consumers.

The BrandPromise

BrandPromise has been covered in great detail in this book, and so it is discussed only briefly here. To become brand-driven, individuals and organizations, regardless of size, must "think like a brand." In many cases, vision or mission statements guide strategic direction and planning. Mission and vision statements typically articulate what a company wants to be or do. The mission statement provides a reason the organization exists and an overall goal. A vision statement gives an overview of the company's purpose, expressing what it *desires* to be. A BrandPromise guides how an organization wants its customers to feel. Figure 10.3 outlines the purpose of a promise.

Mission and vision statements are not necessarily replaced by a promise. Relevant statements and a list of appropriate company values may be quite compatible with a promise. Key ideas or elements from a mission or vision statement could become part of the promise or the brand's principles. Separate mission and vision statements may be phased out when an organization embraces the BrandMindset concept. The promise shows the way—short term and long.

The most important characteristics of an effective BrandPromise are consistency and distinctiveness. Success will never be achieved by making one promise this year and a different one next year. That only confuses everyone: associates, customers, and prospective customers.

FIGURE 10.3

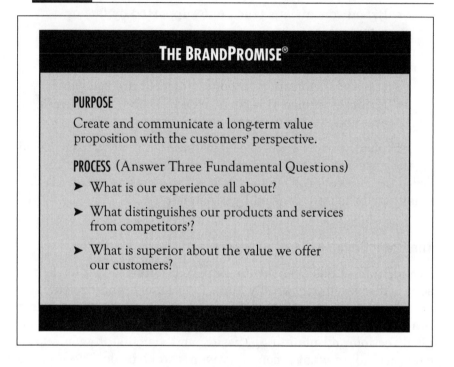

The BrandPromise ensures that customer feelings will be protected and expectations will be met, if not exceeded. To endure, a brand needs to stand for something more, something larger, than a product benefit. Competitors can knock off obvious product and service features—sometimes more economically. However, most competitors who copy a brand's products or services usually do not understand a genuine brand's promise. This is the true competitive advantage of developing and delivering the right promise.

That's the power of a promise.

Brand Blueprint

Successful brands don't happen by accident, and they don't occur overnight. They require a well-thought-out and expertly designed set of plans. When you think of construction, typically images of blueprints and architects come to mind. Buildings, no matter how complex or how simple, follow a set of blueprints that outline all the necessary architectural elements that give the end result its look, feel, and character. The blueprints tell people whether a building is a skyscraper, an office building, or a home, and they say something more. Buildings of all types are designed according to a certain type of style that reflects the taste and personality of their owners. These styles may have historical references or may be very contemporary. Brands are very much the same. Just as distinctive architectural style defines the tone and character of a building, brands are perceived in terms of their architecture.

By now, you understand the importance of "thinking like a brand." The Brand Blueprint is described in Figure 10.4 and is our methodology for constructing and communicating a brand's identity. The *blueprint* can be defined this way:

1. The disciplined, detailed plan required for creating, designing, and communicating the intended brand perception.

2. That which determines the character or style of a brand.

3. A plan that reflects the BrandPromise and outlines the underlying *collective* architecture for the brand name, byline, tagline, graphic representations, and the brand story.

A properly crafted brand creates an aura far greater in perception than the size and value of the business alone. A brand is more than just the actual product and services it is composed of perceived values, characteristics, and attributes that differentiate it from other similar products and services. The important thing to remember is this: *Brand identity exists in the minds of the customers, associates, and influencers.*

If you create the right blueprint for a brand, it's easier to achieve the desired brand perception. Brands serve as an emotional shortcut between a company and its customers. A brand is a picture of the total *experience* in the mind's eye of customers and consumers.

FIGURE 10.4

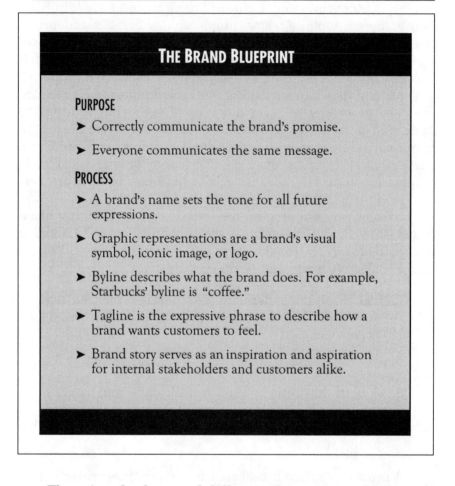

THE BRAND BLUEPRINT

PURPOSE

➤ Correctly communicate the brand's promise.

➤ Everyone communicates the same message.

PROCESS

➤ A brand's name sets the tone for all future expressions.

➤ Graphic representations are a brand's visual symbol, iconic image, or logo.

➤ Byline describes what the brand does. For example, Starbucks' byline is "coffee."

➤ Tagline is the expressive phrase to describe how a brand wants customers to feel.

➤ Brand story serves as an inspiration and aspiration for internal stakeholders and customers alike.

There is a fundamental difference between our blueprint's philosophical approach and traditional marketing practice. In some cases, organizations believe that brand building is the sole function of the marketing department. In these cases, marketers typically take a piecemeal approach to brand building and view each of the components comprising the architecture of a brand as separate and distinct units or variables. We believe that a brand's blueprint should follow a holistic approach.

Implementing the blueprint methodology can optimize a brand's perception, thus enhancing overall brand equity. The Brand Blueprint consists of five basic components:

1. *Brand name:* A unique, memorable, and distinctive name. Nike has become the recognized name in athletic wear. Is there a more distinctive name than Smucker's or Orville Redenbacher? These are people's real names.

2. *Unique graphic representation:* An icon, symbol, or image that graphically depicts the brand's identity. Walt Disney's signature became the company's symbol. Starbucks has its siren, and Target its red bull's-eye.

3. *Byline:* Descriptive words or phrase that tells consumers where to place the brand in their mind's eye—that is, what the brand does. The byline "coffee" accompanies the graphic representation for Starbucks' siren logo and for Ace, it's "hardware."

4. *Tagline:* A message that expresses current functional and emotional benefits to consumers. BMW is the "ultimate driving machine." Crane & Co. is recognized for its superb stationery products. It has a long and storied tradition of quality, producing some of the finest writing papers, greeting cards, and accessories. What can consumers expect when purchasing any of Crane's fine stationery products? Every box of stationery contains an inspiration. Crane's tagline tells consumers: "For the writer somewhere in each of us."

5. *Brand story:* Preserves and communicates the brand's heritage. With Williams-Sonoma, "It all started in the kitchen." Its corporate story is depicted in Figure 10.5.

In our methodology, it takes all five pieces to make a whole. No one piece is more important than the others. They must work in concert with each other. When a balance is struck between all components, a powerful bond is established with customers.

Genuine Every Day: Brand Culturalization

What is the difference between an average brand and a genuine brand? Associates who enthusiastically embrace and *consistently* deliver the organization's BrandPromise every day ultimately spell the difference between mediocre and high performance.

FIGURE 10.5

CUSTOMER SERVICE AND STRONG COMMITMENT TO QUALITY

"The first Williams - Sonoma store opened in 1956, selling a small array of cookware imported from France. Since then, the brand has expanded to hundreds of products from around the world, more than 250 stores nationwide, a direct mail business that distributes millions of catalogs a year, and a highly successful e-commerce site. What has never changed is Williams - Sonoma's dedication to customer service and strong commitment to quality."

—Williams - Sonoma Web site, Company Information

Brands can avoid being average and attain the prestigious status of genuine greatness when everyone throughout the entire organization *lives* the promise.

When an organization aligns its *mindset*, culture, and operations with its brand's principles and values, the promise comes alive. For a genuine brand to be alive in the minds of customers, the organization must be internally focused on delivering the promise through its structure, culture, reward programs, compensation packages, and key activities. Words alone are not enough. Management, at all levels, must be totally committed and demonstrate its commitment to the promise through actions consistent with the organization's values. It is through management's sincere behavior that the promise is reinforced among associates and inspires them to accept the responsibility for delivering the promise to their customers.

Associates are then empowered to do whatever it takes to see that customers' expectations are met. This is how a genuine brand's promise is fulfilled.

Figure 10.6 provides the Brand Culturalization overview.

FIGURE 10.6

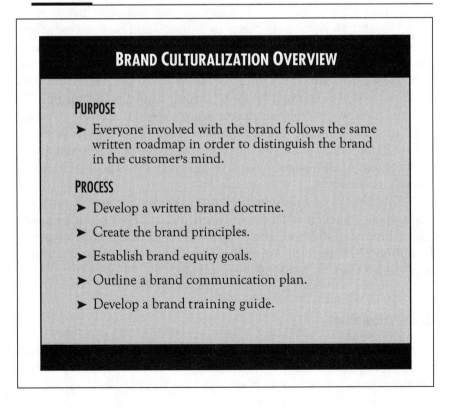

BRAND CULTURALIZATION OVERVIEW

PURPOSE
➤ Everyone involved with the brand follows the same written roadmap in order to distinguish the brand in the customer's mind.

PROCESS
➤ Develop a written brand doctrine.

➤ Create the brand principles.

➤ Establish brand equity goals.

➤ Outline a brand communication plan.

➤ Develop a brand training guide.

Any individual or organization can culturalize its brand's values in a variety of ways to achieve optimum results. For example:

- Use internal communications to nurture morale and build esprit de corps, as well as commitment, through shared vision, mission, values, and principles.
- Provide executives, managers, and associates with a thorough understanding of the BrandPromise and expectations. Train everyone in how to adopt a BrandMindset and how to adapt behavior to "live the brand."
- Demonstrate how processes, practices, and responsibilities are intrinsically linked to delivering the brand's promise to customers.
- Change or modify company policies to ensure that the organization is consistently aligned with its promise. These include training, compensation, rewards, and recruitment.

When associates "buy in" to the fact that the promise is genuine and that management is sincere and committed, they adjust their attitudes and behavior accordingly. The result is a greater degree of satisfaction among both employees and customers, which leads to higher levels of customer retention and preference which in turn leads to strong brand performance.

In a crowded marketplace, where brands compete to be seen and heard, it is the associates who make the difference. Through associates' words and actions, customers learn firsthand if the brand is going to live up to their expectations of a brand's promise.

By offering and delivering a unique promise to differentiate one's brand, backed with an unconditional 100 percent guarantee of total satisfaction, the brand will *earn* a position of privilege among customers, leaving them with the *feeling* of a great experience that builds long-term loyalty.

Brand Advantage

The Brand Advantage methodology is founded on the belief that building a genuine brand is a lifelong, day-in and day-out process. It's not the strategy "du jour" or this year's great idea.

This means that before a strategic plan or a business plan can be prepared, it's necessary to conduct a Brand Assessment or audit to objectively understand how a brand is perceived before an organization can plan where it wants to go. Hence, on a frequent basis and not less than annually, an organization needs to assess how its brand is perceived in the minds of those who matter the most: customers, consumers, associates, influencers, and even shareholders.

Enlightened brands have their finger on the "perceptual pulse" of their key stakeholders every day with samplings of responses and feedback to detect and reinforce positive reactions and to identify and address negative perceptions before they become a trend. It's kind of like balancing a checkbook every month. If you don't do it, by the time there is a problem, it's big!

If an organization is posting its stock price every day, it might be important to add its delighted customers' scores for the day, week, or month.

The other important piece of the Brand Advantage is the constant innovation or the development of a stairway to success. A *stairway to success* is a systematic delivery of product and service advantages to a brand's customers. This is related to the paradigm shift strategy we introduced in Chapter 4. Instead of a one-time innovation, successful brands plan a long-term rollout of future product, service, and experiential improvements that make it difficult for competitors to keep up. This stairway to success involves a plan for a coordinated and consistent approach to improvements that enhance customer experiences.

THOUGHT GUIDE

PROMISE PERSPECTIVES

- One question must be constantly asked and answered by each and every person associated with a brand: What's our promise, and how do I deliver it?
- The following conditions must be present in an organization in order to develop a genuine brand:
  1. The organization must embrace a customer-centric philosophy.

2. A proven scientific methodology must be utilized to develop an effective promise.

3. Every person associated with the organization needs to be passionate about delivering the promise.

- A genuine brand should be "aspirational" and should invoke a positive feeling as well as a sense of pride. The genuine brand process should be focused on identifying, communicating, and delivering a brand's distinctive characteristics, those that are important and beneficial to its stakeholders and especially to its customers and prospective customers.

- The secret is to select or develop distinctive attributes that a brand's customers and prospective customers will value the most and seek out the brand for.

- Success will be achieved by making and delivering one promise over the long term.

- A properly crafted brand creates an aura far greater in perception than the size and value of the business alone. A brand is more than just the actual product and services; it is composed of perceived values, functional characteristics, and emotional attributes that differentiate it from other similar products and services.

- When an organization aligns its *mindset*, culture, and operations with its brand's principles and values, the promise comes alive.

- Enlightened brands have their finger on the "perceptual pulse" of their key stakeholders every day with samplings of responses and feedback. They need to understand positive perceptions, and they need to understand negative perceptions before they become a trend.

ENDNOTES

PREFACE

1. "What High-Tech Managers Need to Know about Brands," *Harvard Business Review*, July–August 1999.

CHAPTER 1

1. Tony Simons, *The Integrity Dividend* (San Francisco, CA: Jossey-Bass, to be published in 2008).
2. Ibid.
3. Steve Fisher, "Landing a Legacy," *Costco Connection*, September 2007, p. 19.
4. Ibid., p. 18.
5. Rob Rush, "Top of Mind: Let's Operationalize the Brand Promise," www.brandweek.com, March 21, 2005.
6. Paul Scott, "When Good Knees Go Bad," *Runner's World,* March 2007, p. 72.
7. Rick Hendrie, "Your Experience Is the Brand," *Hotel Online*, November 2004.
8. Donald N. Sull and Charles Spinosa, "Promise-Based Management," *Harvard Business Review*, April 2007, pp. 79–80.

CHAPTER 2

1. Linda Tischler, "Hospitality Sweet," interview with Danny Meyer, *Fast Company,* September 2006, p.30.
2. "Poor Customer Service Drive Nearly Half of U.S. Consumers to Take Their Business Elsewhere, Accenture Survey Finds," Accenture Survey, August 7, 2007.

3. Chuck Salter, "The Agonies of Lewis Black," *Fast Company,* September 2006, p. 64.

4. Tim Sanders, Likeability Factor Seminar, 2006.

5. Tony Peju, Peju Wines letter, November 20, 2006.

6. Dale Carnegie, *How to Win Friends and Influence People* (New York: Simon & Schuster, 1964), p. 27.

7. Ibid., p. 103.

8. Linda Kaplan Thaler and Robin Koval, *The Power of Nice* (New York: Doubleday, 2006), p. xiii.

9. Dave Carpenter, "Ray Griffith, Ace Hardware Thinks Outside the Big Boxes," *Seattle Times,* January 24, 2007, p. E2.

10. "JD Power Ranking for Ace Hardware for Highest Customer Satisfaction," *USA Today*, June 29, 2007.

11. www.wolfermans.com/store/about_our_products, accessed on February 7, 2007.

12. Catherine Arnold, "Satisfaction's the Name of the Game," *Marketing News*, October 15, 2004, p. 45.

13. *The Costco Connection*, November 2006, p. 71.

14. Letter to Shareholders, Costco annual report, 2006.

CHAPTER 3

1. "What High-Tech Managers Need to Know about Brands," *Harvard Business Review*, July–August 1999.

2. Christine Born, "Brand-Name Product Power Deeply Rooted in the Brain: Study," www.cbc.ca, November 2006.

3. Ed Haidenthaller, "Did Your Last Merger or Acquisition Optimize Returns?" *Boardroom Briefing— Mergers and Acquisitions*, Summer 2007, p. 8.

4. Northwestern Mutual annual report, 2006.

5. Ibid.

6. Tina Goodwin, "Learn to Hear the Voice of the Consumer," *Marketing News*, May 1, 2007, p. 23.

7. Husqvarna Product Guide, 2006.

8. Bruce Wallin, "Crystal Persuasion," *Robb Report*, November 2006, p. 284.

9. Harley-Davidson annual report, 2006, p. 6.

CHAPTER 4

1. Byron Acohido, "Amazon Won't Go Down with the Ship," *USA Today*, July 30,2007, Money Section, p. 1B.

2. Eric Krell, "Branding Together," *HR Magazine*, October 2006, p.50.

3. Ibid.

4. Donald N. Sull and Charles Spinosa, "Promise-Based Management," *Harvard Business Review*, April 2007, p. 86.

5. Ibid.

6. Ibid.

7. Tina Goodwin, "Change It All Around," *Marketing News,* May 1, 2007, p. 20.

8. Strativity Group, Inc., "Random Sampling," *Marketing News*, April 2007, p. 3.

9. John Yokyama, "The World Famous Pike Place Fish Story," *Anderson Retailing Issues Newsletter*, vol. 13, no. 6, November 2001.

10. "Building Better Boards," Heidrick & Struggles, John T. Gardner (2005).

11. McKinsey quarterly survey of 1,026 corporate directors, January 2005, p. 50.

12. Dave Ulrich and Norm Smallwood, "Building a Leadership Brand," *Harvard Business Review*, July–August 2007, p. 98.

13. Duane Knapp, "Independent Annual Customer Audits Should Be Required by Every Board of Directors," *Corporate Board Member Magazine Online*, June 2005.

14. Michael Treacy, "Innovation," *Marketing News*, February 2007, p. 19.

15. Outlook Special Excerpt, *Forbes*, May 7, 2007.

16. Darryl Owens, "Innovation Requires Change in Approach," *Marketing News*, March 2007, p. 20.

17. Ibid.

18. Arthur Markowitz, "From Roseville to Greatland, Target Still Hits the Mark," *Discount Store News*, November 2006. p. 1.

19. Ibid.

20. Ibid.

21. Ibid.

22. Ibid., p. 2.

23. Ibid., p. 3.

CHAPTER 5

1. Langberg, "Mail-In Rebates Not Dying Fast Enough," San Jose *Mercury News*, July 10, 2006.

2. Alina Tugend, "Short Cuts; A Growing Anger Over Unpaid Rebates," *New York Times*, March 4, 2006.

3. Sid Kirchheimer, "Scam Alert: Rebate Runaround," *AARP Bulletin*, June 2007.

4. Eric Bangerman, "CompUSA Forced to Pay Overdue Rebates," www.arstechnica.com, March 14, 2005.

5. Brian Grow, "The Great Rebate Runaround," *BusinessWeek Online,* November 2005.

6. Chris Serres, "More Electronics Buyers Skip Extended Warranties," *Seattle Times*, Business and Technology section, July 14, 2007.

7. Ibid.

8. Graham W. Galloway and Dale E. Jones, "12 Crucial People Questions for Directors," *Boardroom Briefing: Mergers and Acquisitions,* Fall 2006, p. 18.

9. David Pinto, "Retailer Learns What's in a Name," *Mass Market Retailer*, February 12, 2007, p. 8.

10. Ibid.

11. Joe Calloway, "Customer Service Hall of Shame," *MSN Money*, April 26, 2007.

12. Laura Petrecca, "Stores, Banks Go Speedy to Win Harried Customers," *USA Today*, Money section, December 1, 2006.

13. Jayne O'Donnell and Elaine Hughes, "Sometimes, Good Customer Service Depends on the Customer," *USA Today*, July 6, 2007, p. 3B.

14. www.seattle.gov/cable/2001_Bill-OF-Rights.

CHAPTER 6

1. Del Quentin Wilber, "Gerald Grinstein Helped Pull Delta Out of Nose Dive," *Seattle Times*, July 29, 2007, Business and Technology section, p 66.

2. Rhonda Byrne, *The Secret* (New York: Atria Books, 2006), pp. 81 and 86.

3. Ibid.

4. Ranjay Gulati, "Silo Busting: How to Execute on the Promise of Customer Focus," *Harvard Business Review*, May 2007, p. 98.

5. Edward Iwata, "Businesses Grow More Socially Conscious," *USA Today*, February 14, 2007, p. 3B.

6. Ibid.

7. Bill Gates, "Business @ the Speed of Thought," *Business Plus*, May 15, 2000, p. 200.

8. www.zappos.com/about, accessed on August 19, 2007.

CHAPTER 7

1. Destination Marketing International, Meeting Professional supplement, February 2007, p. 29.

2. Tom Lowry, "The CEO Mayor," *BusinessWeek*, June 25, 2007, p. 58.

3. Roger Yu, "Fliers Pick Las Vegas McCarran as Favorite Airport," *USA Today*, Travel section, June 30, 2006.
4. The author wishes to thank Sarah Kirby Yung and Tourism Vancouver for their contribution.

CHAPTER 8

1. Peter Montoya, *The Brand Called You* (Personal Branding Press, 2002), Foreword, p. 2.
2. Ibid.
3. www.masters.org/en_US/news/tournament, Bob Jones, Jr., Augusta National Golf Club comment, April 1967.
4. Tom Cunneff, "The Shark's New Waters," *Links Magazine*, March 2007, p. 58.
5. Ibid., p. 60.
6. Ibid.
7. Ibid., p. 58.
8. Ibid.
9. Greg Norman with Don T. Phillips, *The Way of the Shark* (New York: Atria Books, 2006), p. 317.
10. Liza Hamm and Michelle Tauber, "All the Dish," *People Magazine*, May 14, 2007, p. 122.
11. Katie Hafner, "Wielding Kitchen Knives and Honing Office Skills," *New York Times*, Business section, January 12, 2007.
12. "Every Day with Rachael Ray," *Rach's Notebook*, January 2007.
13. Ibid.
14. Hamm and Tauber, "All the Dish," p. 120.
15. Jeff Meisner, "Pro Numbers; Athletes Score in Likeability Survey," *Puget Sound Business Journal*, June 3–July 6, 2006, p. 3.

CHAPTER 9

1. Mary Lower, "Four Tips Help Authentic Marketing to Nonprofits," *Marketing News*," June 15, 2007, p. 12.
2. Ibid.
3. Elaine Fogel, "Invest in the Future by Branding the Organization," *Marketing New*s, June 15, 2007, p. 13.
4. Anne Field, "Making a Little Company Look Big," *The New York Times*, Technology section, July 2, 2007.
5. Barbara Basler, "Good Rapport Is Good Medicine," *AARP Bulletin*, November 2006, p. 22.

BRAND INDEX

For your convenience, we have provided the URLs for the following list of selected brands that are referenced throughout the book.

CHAPTER 1

AAA	www.AAA.com
J.D. Power	www.jdpower.com
Ketel One Vodka	www.ketelone.com
Restaurants Unlimited	www.r-u-i.com
Southwest Airlines	www.southwest.com
Starbucks	www.starbucks.com

CHAPTER 2

Ace Hardware	www.acehardware.com
Consumer Reports	www.consumerreports.org
Costco	www.costco.com
Microsoft	www.microsoft.com
New York Life Insurance	www.newyorklife.com
Peju Wines	www.peju.com
State Farm Insurance	www.statefarm.com
Sunset Magazine	www.sunset.com
Wolferman's	www.wolfermans.com

CHAPTER 3

Haggen Food & Pharmacy	www.haggen.com
Husqvarna	www.husqvarna.com
In-N-Out	www.in-n-out.com
Long's Drugs	www.longs.com
Mayo Clinic	www.mayoclinic.com
Northwestern Mutual Life Insurance Co.	www.nmfn.com
Riedel	www.riedel.com
RK Dixon	www.rkdixon.com

CHAPTER 4

Bartell Hotels	www.bartellhotels.com
Ginn Reunion Resort	www.reunionresort.com
Nordstrom	www.nordstrom.com
Pike Place Market	www.pikeplacemarket.com
Target	www.target.com

CHAPTER 5

American Express	www.americanexpress.com
AutoSport	www.autosport.com
Doctors Eyecare Network	www.doctorseyecare.com
JetBlue	www.jetblue.com
Nordstrom	www.nordstrom.com

CHAPTER 6

American Express	www.americanexpress.com
FedEx	www.fedex.com
Google	www.google.com
3M	www.3m.com
Ziploc	www.ziploc.com

CHAPTER 7

Certified Tourism Ambassador	www.tourismambassador institute.com
Destination Marketing Association International	www.destination marketing.org
Indian Wells	www.indianwells.com
Las Vegas	www.visitlasvegas.com
New York City	www.nycvisit.com
Santa Monica Convention & Visitors Bureau	www.santamonica.com
Tourism Vancouver	www.tourismvancouver.com
Walt Disney Company	www.disney.com

CHAPTER 8

Bruce Blomgren	www.bruceblomgren.com
Hall Wines	www.hallwines.com
JT's Original Bar-B-Que	www.jtbbq.com
Greg Norman	www.shark.com
Rachael Ray	www.rachaelraymag.com
Annika Sorenstam	www.annikasorenstam.com

CHAPTER 9

Callison Architecture	www.callison.com
Destination Marketing	www.destination
Association International	marketing.org
Heart Rhythm Society	www.hrsonline.org
Make-A-Wish Foundation	www.wish.org
SAFE Credit Union	www.safecu.org

INDEX

ABOUT THE AUTHOR

Duane Knapp is recognized as the authority on building genuine brands and the BrandPromise philosophy. He is the chairman and founder of BrandStrategy, Inc., which has advised over 300 brands in 14 countries worldwide including corporations, communities, societies, professional associations, institutions, countries, world-class professionals, celebrities, and individuals who desire to optimize their perception, image, and success.

He has served on dozens of organizations' boards of directors and has held a variety of senior executive positions, including chief executive officer, president, executive vice president, vice president of corporate marketing, vice president corporate development, and corporate strategist at several public and private companies. These include Westin Hotels (Westin Enterprises and Discoveries retail stores and catalogs), Holiday Corporation (Holiday Inn and Holiday Clubs, Perkins Family Restaurants), The Promus Companies (Embassy Suites, Residence Inn, Hampton Inn, Homewood Suites, and Harrah's Casinos), and Cinnabon World Famous Cinnamon Rolls. He advises leading law firms relating to high-profile brand and intellectual property matters and has specific expertise in the fields of travel and hospitality, food and beverage products, restaurants, retailing, health care, financial services, and real estate development. He has been approved as a senior gaming officer by both the New Jersey and Las Vegas Gaming Authorities.

Mr. Knapp has taught and lectured widely at universities and graduate schools throughout the United States, including Vanderbilt, Stanford, the University of California, the University of Colorado at Boulder, and Seattle University. He is the leading keynote speaker on the subject of building genuine brands and has been published, quoted, or featured in hundreds of publications, including *BusinessWeek, Brandweek, CFO Magazine, Association Management, Marketing, Washington CEO, Bankers Magazine, Design Forum, Focus Magazine, Risk Management, Forbes Magazine Travel, Distribution Reports, Private Clubs Magazine, International Journal of Medical Marketing, The*

Seattle Times, and *The Journal of Commerce*, as well as in many private corporate and association publications and on television and radio talk shows.

His first book, *The BrandMindset*®, was published by McGraw-Hill and was selected by IBM and American Express as the "must read" book for their top 400 executives. Available in seven languages, it is considered to be the definitive guide to building genuine brands. Mr. Knapp is also the coauthor of *Destination BrandScience,* the guidebook for developing genuine brands for communities and destinations, published by the Destination Marketing Association International.

Duane Knapp's BrandPromise® philosophy is highly acclaimed and has been extensively referenced and quoted in many books and publications including Tim Sanders' bestseller, *Love Is the Killer App*; Michael Levine's *A Branded World*; and David Aaker's *Building Strong Brands*. He also wrote the foreword for *License to Serve*.

Mr. Knapp received his BA in business administration from Western Michigan University and his MBA from the University of Toledo. He also completed a postgraduate program in strategic marketing at the Stanford University Graduate School of Business.

He can be contacted at www.brandstrategy.com.